CHURCH SOCIAL WORK

CHURCH SOCIAL WORK

HELPING THE WHOLE PERSON
IN THE CONTEXT OF THE CHURCH

Edited by
DIANA S. RICHMOND GARLAND

CONTENTS

In Appreciation

This book would not have been possible without the prayerful support, friendship, and encouragement of the board members of the North American Association of Christians in Social Work. The combination of a deep and abiding Christian faith and its expression in a commitment to the social work profession in these good people has provided inspiration and energy for this volume. The love and care expressed and felt in this group for one another as individuals and as an organization, regardless of denominational and philosophical differences, has embodied for me Jesus' commandment to love one another. I am grateful.

For the twelve years I have been privileged to work with her, Dean C. Anne Davis of the Carver School of Church Social Work has not wavered in her commitment to developing a strong curriculum and school for the education of church social workers. The faculty of the School has been equally tireless and committed. I am honored to call them colleagues and friends. Some of them have provided chapters for this volume. All have provided encouragement and the vision that this book needed to be a volume that crossed denominations rather than written only by and for Southern Baptists.

The privilege of working with students called of God and committed to caring for "the least of these" has given our faculty the joy of watching our work bear fruit beyond what we could have imagined. Jane Ferguson, one of our alumni, describes that fruit in her chapter and gives depth to our understanding of church social work.

We are only one small piece in the mosaic of church social work. The other authors in this volume bear testimony to the breadth and diversity of this field of practice. One of the joys of working on this volume has been developing and strengthening relationships with all the authors. They have been patient with the seemingly unending cycles of editing that were necessary to weave the chapters into this volume.

David Sherwood has been an outstanding editor, encouraging from the outset that we attempt a book of this nature. It would not have been written without his support.

God has been at work in our midst. Thanks be to God.

Diana Garland
Louisville, KY
June 6, 1991

CHAPTER 1

Church Social Work: An Introduction

by Diana S. Richmond Garland*

The social work profession has grown in many directions since its beginnings in the settlement houses and missions of churches, denominational agencies, and voluntary services of individual Christians, but social workers have continued to serve as the hands and hearts of the church in outreach to oppressed and hurting persons. The church was the first and has continued to be a prominent context for social work practice, joined more recently by government assistance programs, schools, hospitals and clinics, mental health agencies, industry, and most recently, the for-profit private service sector. Almost 9% of social workers who were members of the National Association of Social Workers, and who responded to a 1982 survey, were practicing under sectarian auspices (National Association of Social Workers, 1985).

The Historical Development of Church Social Work

The church and its ministries provided the seedbed for the development of the social work profession. Almost all modern social services can be traced back to roots in religious organizations. Johnson has noted that the church was the "mother of social work" (1941, p. 404). Long before the social work profession's birth, the church concerned itself with the needs of persons, particularly poor, oppressed, and marginalized persons. In a helpful article, E. Glenn Hinson describes the historical involvement of the church in social ministries prior to the Reformation (1988). In the first three centuries of the Christian era, Christians amazed the world around them with the extent to which they ministered to the needs of others, especially those who had no one else to care for them. Hippolytus, around C.E. 217, considered care of widows as a test for baptism. The early church took on the major task of caring for abandoned and orphaned children who had been left on waste heaps to die, taking them into their own homes or creating foundling homes.

*Diana Garland, ACSW, Ph.D., is Associate Professor of Social Work, Carver School of Church Social Work, and Director of the Gheens Center for Christian Faith Ministry, The Southern Baptist Theological Seminary, Louisville, Kentucky.

Early Christians sought to ransom slaves, some even by voluntarily placing themselves in bondage. Within the fellowship of the church, class distinctions ceased to have meaning. Converts who had to leave their occupations to join the fellowship (e.g., gladiators, actors, and prostitutes) were given work by wealthy members or provided support from a common fund (Hinson, 1988).

From the beginning, Christians have created institutions to meet human needs. The *agape*, a fellowship meal for the hungry, began as a part of the Eucharist but soon became a separate observance in private homes and public gatherings. With Constantine's conversion to Christianity came major funding for a wide range of church ministries. The church became more deeply involved in the care of orphans and foundlings, increasingly encouraging Christians to adopt these children. It was taken for granted that the church would care for the poor. Churches and individual church members established hospitals. Monasteries gave employment to many, more for the purpose of giving aid than for the work they could do. During the medieval period, social service was left, for the most part, in the hands of the church. Monasteries continued to serve as centers of charity and fed the hungry during famine and war (Hinson, 1988).

Throughout the Reformation and the modern period (1500 to present), the church began to reexamine its attitudes toward poverty, social welfare, and family life, even as it continued to care for the poor and the oppressed. In an excellent companion article to Glenn Hinson's article, Bill J. Leonard has described the role of the modern church in social ministries and social action (1988). He points out that the early English Puritans frequently criticized the social and economic abuses of the seventeenth century. They condemned landlords who charged excessive rents and wealthy persons who ignored the needs of the poor. The New England Puritans looked forward to a day when the existing social order would be transformed into the image of the Kingdom of God. Even so, they took punitive action against groups and persons considered criminal, including Baptists and Quakers, using torture, imprisonment, banishment, and execution.

Quakers also had a significant influence on church thought during the early years of the country. Leonard (1988) describes the Quaker doctrine of the "inner light" as the basis for an immense valuing of all persons, who should be treated accordingly. Quaker egalitarianism supported pacifism, care for the poor, prison reform, reforms in care for the mentally ill and disabled, and opposition to slavery. For example, John Woolman (1700-1772) traveled throughout the American South convincing

Quakers to manumit their slaves, to work toward legislation banning further importation of slaves, and to boycott the products of slave labor (Leonard, 1988).

During the eighteenth and nineteenth centuries, according to Leonard, church groups and individuals formed voluntary societies, often as a result of religious awakenings. Denominations were also developing agencies to which they assigned various social ministries. These societies and agencies addressed the problems of hunger, slum life, unemployment, mental illness, disabilities, prison reform, and the care of widows and orphans. Alcoholism became recognized as a cause of family violence, poverty, and disease. In the early 1800s, temperance societies became the temperance movement, the birthplace of American feminism (Leonard, 1988). At the same time, the debate over slavery divided denominations and Christians.

Timothy Smith has said that the rapid growth of concern with social issues such as poverty, workers' rights, liquor and alcoholism, prison reform, slum housing, and racial bitterness chiefly distinguished the American churches after 1865 from that of the early part of the century (Smith, 1976). With the founding in 1850 of the Five Points Mission in New York City by Phoebe Palmer, a holiness evangelist, Protestant institutional ministries in the slums of the nation began (Smith, 1976).

The term "social gospel" was first used in 1886 by Iowa Congregationalist minister Charles O. Brown (Leonard, 1988) and became the label for that era's efforts toward Christianizing the social order. Walter Rauschenbusch (1861-1918), a German Baptist pastor, despaired of individualized attempts at social service because he saw that they perpetuated the corrupt social system; his church in New York City was located on the edge of Hell's Kitchen. He became the leader of the social gospel movement, later articulating the basis for the movement in his writing as a professor at Rochester Theological Seminary. He believed that the Kingdom of God provided the model of society ((Leonard, 1988). "The Social Gospel movement represented a significant effort to call the church to respond to the social problems of the industrial age and a recognition of the corporate nature of both sin and redemption" (Leonard, 1988, p. 250). The Social Gospel movement attempted to provide a Christian theological basis for social concern and social action and was the impetus for the development of the extensive structure of sectarian agencies which still fill a significant role in the social service system of American cities.

Churches were far from unified in their understanding of the role of the church in Christian concerns, however. Some church leaders, such

3

as Dwight Moody (1837-1899) and Billy Sunday (1863-1935), opposed involvement in social issues, believing it to be a distraction from what they considered to be the church's real mission, which is to win souls (Loewenberg, 1988). The idea for dividing the poor into "deserving" and "undeserving" can be attributed to some Christians' interpretation and application of 2 Thessalonians 3:10b: "If anyone will not work, neither let him eat." (*NASV*). For example, Cotton Mather (1663-1728), one of the most influential preachers in American history, urged his congregation to engage constantly in doing good, but to support only poor people who were worthy of charity (Loewenberg, 1988).

In the midst of this ferment, the social work profession was developing. Some Christians began to choose social work as the expression of their understanding of this mission: Owen R. Lovejoy started his career as a minister and later became a leading social work executive and social reformer; Jane Addams rejected a missionary career to become a pioneer social worker. Some were attempting to hold the two–church and social work–together. For example, Maud Reynolds McClure, who had lived in a settlement house in New York City and studied at the New York School of Philanthropy (later Columbia University School of Social Work), began a settlement house in Louisville, Kentucky, and began teaching social work courses in 1912 in the Baptist Woman's Missionary Union Training School, later to become the Carver School of Church Social Work of the Southern Baptist Theological Seminary.

Since those early years of the social work profession, the relationship between church and the social work profession has been dramatically uneven, ranging from collaboration to mutual disinterest or disdain. It has varied over time, communities, situations, and with particular social workers and churches. Social workers have viewed churches as any one or a mixture of the following: significant community resources, dangerous organizations which foster dysfunctional coping in clients, powerful reactionary groups calling for perpetuation of a status quo that oppresses and marginalizes certain groups, voices for constructive societal action to change the status quo, an institution so irrelevant to the work of the social work profession that its role in client's lives is ignored, a profoundly significant source of informal social support and existential hope in the lives of client.

Whatever social workers' attitudes toward it may be, however, the church continues to be a significant and influential institution–for good or for ill–in this nation's formal social services and, to an even greater extent, in the informal social support and services available to persons and their families. Perhaps with the exception of public schools, con-

4

gregations reach more families than any other institution in the United States; 40% of families attend one of the nation's 335,000 congregations in a typical week, and 70% attend worship services in a month's time (National Crime Prevention Council, 1990). Churches are the largest providers of preschool child care in the country (Freeman, 1986) and have unique access to even more homes through informal societal networks.

What is Church Social Work?

Moberg defines the church as "organized religion," which includes all organizations seeking to develop, renew, and guide persons' religious lives (Moberg, 1984, p. 1). The church is by definition a social organization, with a structure based on a division of responsibility and privilege between persons, tasks to be performed, and defined processes, rules, and norms for performing them. It has a body of beliefs codified in creeds and doctrines. Members identify with one another and with the organization. Despite variations in structures, from large and complex to small and simple, from highly formalized to highly informal, from autocratic to democratic, all churches are groups of people acting together on behalf of religious interests. "Any organization or association of persons striving to perpetuate or propagate some religious belief or ideal is a church" (Moberg, 1984, p. 16). To this sociological definition one might add from an insider's perspective that a church is such an organization or association which defines the religious beliefs or ideals it is perpetuating or propagating as Christian, however the organization or association may define that term.

As a context for social work practice, the church and church agency remain distinctively different from other settings for professional practice (Garland & Conrad, 1990). Church social workers bring the social work profession's knowledge, values, and skills to the church as a resource. They help the church understand the needs of persons, define those needs as a ministry challenge central to the mission of the church, and equip church members for effective service and/or social action. For example, in response to the problems of homelessness in a church's community, a church social worker educates the church about the complex of factors that create homelessness. The social worker guides the church in a study of the response of the people of God to homelessness in the Bible and in the history of the church, and a study of the theological ramifications of responses the church can make. Finally, if the church decides to involve itself, the social worker helps the church develop programs of ministry to homeless persons and action plans for speaking out on the societal issues that place persons and families at risk for homelessness.

Christian social ministry refers to "the activities carried out by redeemed individuals called by God to proclaim the good news to minister to the needy, and to seek justice for all" (Davis, 1983, p. 523). It is the work and mission of the church, of all Christians. Church social work provides professional leadership and expertise, when they are needed, for this work. Sometimes, church social work provides guidance and consultation to the social ministry and social action programs of the church, as in the development and administration of programs which link families at risk of homelessness with church congregations who can provide needed material and social supports, and which encourage church members to involve themselves in addressing the social problems which contribute to homelessness. Church social workers also use their expertise to represent the church in ministry and social action. For example, a social worker in the church-sponsored shelter for homeless families provides case management and crisis intervention services for individual families and advocates for legislative initiatives that will increase the availability of low-income housing.

Unlike the professional social worker in a community agency, the church social worker has as a primary task the equipping of others–the people of God–to serve. Although they serve clients directly, they cannot do this *in place of* the ministry of the church. *Ministry* is a personal all-encompassing calling to a lifestyle; it is not a profession that can be limited to workdays and from which one can retire (Garland, 1988). Church members are the primary ministers. Findley Edge has argued, "A lay person cannot pay someone else to fulfill his or her ministry for God" (1983, p. 23). Even the church social worker employed in a highly professionalized position, such as providing family therapy services for children who have been placed in residential care and their families, has a role, whether recognized or not, in linking the community of faith in caring ways with families in crisis. That linkage may be one of supportive friendships for a family isolated in their crisis, of respite care for a family who has no one to help them with the daily responsibility of a child with special needs, or of material assistance during a time of financial crisis. Hessel (1982) concludes, "The primary role of professional church workers is to equip a faithful *community* to intervene compassionately in the social system and to enhance caring interpersonal relations in ways that are consistent with Christian maturity" (p. 125).

6

Several characteristics distinguish the church setting from other contexts for social work practice and define the nature of church social work (Garland & Conrad, 1990). First, church social work takes place in the context of a voluntary organization. Church social workers often relate not only to the organization which employs them but also to other levels of church organization. The social worker in a denominational agency spends significant amounts of time consulting, speaking, and developing resources in churches. Social workers employed on the staff of a congregation must deal with denominational policies and programs that affect their work and the social issues of the community. In all the church settings for social work practice, the social worker must respond to a constituency of small voluntary groups who wield power that can be both supportive and oppressive.

Second, church social work takes place as a secondary function in a host organization, much like medical social work or school social work. Even so, when the church social worker understands the mission of the church and can articulate the theological ramifications of the social issues of the day, social ministry and social action become indispensable ways for the church to pursue its calling. Unlike the social service agency, however, the church has other equally significant tasks–worship, fellowship, evangelism. Its mission is to proclaim the Good News and to serve as a living witness to the love of God as shown in the life, death, and resurrection of Jesus Christ. Social ministry and social action are indispensable functions of evangelism (Miles, 1988) as well as ministry in their own right.

Third, the role of lay persons is central in church social work. Christians are called to serve, whether or not the service leads to conversion of those served. Social ministry is doing deeds of love and mercy–feeding the hungry, clothing the naked, visiting the sick and imprisoned (Matt. 25:31-46). Social action involves attempts to change social structures, including advocating in behalf of justice for the oppressed. Social ministry often leads to social action as an attempt to change the forces that create the needs that require social ministry. Instead of helping poor families pay exorbitant utility bills, a church becomes involved in lobbying for legislation that will limit utility bills to a fixed percentage of income, or for legislation requiring landlords to weatherize low income rental properties. Delos Miles says that the story of the Samaritan in Luke 10:25-37 illustrates the difference between social ministry and social action. What the Samaritan did was social ministry. If he had sought to change the conditions which led to robbing and mugging on the Jericho road, that would have been social action (Miles, 1988). Clearly, church social work needs to lead the church both in social ministry and in social action.

Fourth, the church serves as a mediating structure in our society, one which, like the family, stands between individuals and the large institutions of public life. It mediates, or serves as a buffer, that protects persons and families from having to deal with these large social institutions alone (Garland & Conrad, 1990). For example, individuals in a neighborhood turn to the church for advocacy with a local government considering changing zoning ordinances so that neighborhood restaurants can serve alcohol. In the sanctuary movement, churches have become advocates in behalf of voiceless political refugees (Bau, 1985).

Finally, churches have a culture of their own. Like families, churches come with many different structures and ways of living and defining themselves. They have decision-making processes that vary from highly formal structures and hierarchies to informal, democratic, fluid processes. They have historical identities that shape their current understanding of themselves; these identities reflect not only denominational heritage but also the unique histories of particular communities and the interweaving of the church with the events and development of the church's surrounding social and physical environment. Also like families, churches develop over time, going through organizational stages that partially shape their current response to the human needs and resources within and outside itself (Moberg, 1984).

The church social worker needs to be able to operate within and use the language and cultural patterns of the church community; the Bible, theology, and Christian values and lifestyle serve as foundation and resources for practice. For example, Biblical concepts of forgiveness, confession, and repentance can provide a foundation for helping Christians work through family conflict. The concepts of the family of God and Christian hospitality provide the ground for social action in behalf of homeless and isolated persons and social ministry programs that strive to include them in the life of the community.

Understanding these distinctive characteristics of the church context is just as important for effective social work practice as is understanding the culture, history, and current life experiences of an ethnic family requesting family services. Whether a small congregation or a large denominational agency, an assessment of the context for church social work practice calls for sensitivity and specialized knowledge.

The Difference between Church Social Work and Christian Social Work

Frank Loewenberg (1988) has commented that there seem to be two types of social workers, one group basing their practice on secular, humanist principles rooted in the positivist scientific tradition and another group whose practice is based on religious beliefs and values. Considerable misunderstanding, mistrust, and alienation exist between these two different groups. Martin Marty (1980) has wondered if there are two types of social work, "godly" and "godless." To confuse matters more, there is a group between these two, Christians who base their professional social work practice on both religious faith and science. They believe that human interpretation of God's revelation through the created natural world via the scientific method is equal and complementary to human interpretation of God's revelation in the written Word (Farnsworth, 1981).

Church social work cuts across the entire continuum from integration to segregation of faith-based and science-based professional social work practice. Church social work is not delimited by the personal faith of the social worker, nor by the extent to which that faith is related to professional practice. Instead, it is defined by the context in which the social worker is practicing. Many social workers in church settings see their practice as based primarily on their faith, using professional social work knowledge and skills as they see fit; many others integrate their personal faith with their professional practice, drawing from both and struggling with the tensions that may consequently be created. Still others separate faith from practice: some social workers employed in church contexts are not Christians; others view their personal faith and church membership as separate from their professional practice.

"Social work" designates a profession and is qualified–specialized–by the contexts in which it is practiced (e.g., school social work, medical or health social work, church social work) or by the populations it serves (social work with groups, the aging, children and youth, the church and its community). It is not specialized by the personal belief and value system or organizing life principles of the individual professional; there is no such thing as Christian social work, Jewish social work, or Marxist social work. We speak of Christian physicians, but not Christian medicine, and Christian farmers, but not Christian agriculture (Garland, 1986). In summary, church social work is a practice specialization, a context for practice, not a value and belief system of the professional. Social workers are employed as staff members and consultants by congregations; in community, child welfare, and mental health agencies sponsored by single congregations, denominations, and ecumenical groups of churches; in international settings; and as clinicians, community organizers, consultants, program developers, administrators, and advocates.

The Literature of Church Social Work

For many reasons, church social workers have not spilled much ink writing about their practice. First of all, there has been little professional recognition that practice in churches and church agencies is distinctive enough to deserve recognition as a unique context for practice. Instead of identifying the church as a unique practice context, social workers have often looked for the similarities and shared concerns of their practice with that of social workers in other settings. After all, church social work takes many different forms, from clinical services in treatment agencies to community center programming. For example, those involved in community ministries have had the work of community organizing as a reference, and those in the residential children's homes and other children's services of the church have looked to and been incorporated into the social work specialization of child welfare.

Secondly, many social workers in clearly identifiable church contexts, such as members of congregational staffs, have often seen their role as a dual professional identity rather than a unique social work specialization. This dual identity has been reinforced by degree programs in which students receive a divinity or Christian education degree from a seminary which contains some social work courses. They then complete a social work master's degree in a university that accepts the seminary coursework as meeting part of their degree requirements. With the two degrees from different schools come two professional identities which the social worker/church leader is left to integrate and/or hold in tension with one another.

Church social work gained formal recognition as a specialization by the social work profession (and by theological education) with the establishment of the Carver School of Church Social Work of The Southern Baptist Theological Seminary in 1984, and the accreditation of its Master of Social Work degree in 1987 by the Commission on Accreditation of the Council on Social Work Education. The faculty of this school has begun to develop the literature in church social work through their recent publications (e.g., Davis, 1983, 1988; Escobar, 1988; Garland, 1985, 1986, 1987, 1988; Garland & Bailey, 1990; Garland & Conrad, 1990; Garland & Pancoast, 1990; Rainbow, 1988; and Walker, 1988).

Finally, church social workers have probably written little about their practice because they have been too busy practicing to take the time to reflect and write about what they do. Church social workers are unique people. They commit themselves to being the heart and hands of the church in ministry to those in need. They find it hard, therefore, to pull back from the work and construct the islands of reflection necessary to evaluate and write about what they do.

By contrast, much more has been written on the Christian social ministries of the church (e.g., Conrad, 1980; Delamarter, 1970; Hessel, 1982; Johnson, 1977; Joseph & Conrad, 1988; Morris, 1986; Pinson, 1971). Others have written on Christian faith and social work practice (e.g., Keith-Lucas, 1960, 1972, 1985; Loewenberg, 1988; Marty, 1980; Spencer, 1956).

We have written this book to define more specifically the church as a context for social work practice, or rather, as a mosaic of contexts for practice–from the social worker employed by a congregation to provide consultation for developing social ministries in its community to the social worker employed by denominational and ecumenical agencies which are international in their scope. Rather than attempt to provide a comprehensive literature review in this introductory chapter, each chapter in the volume will examine the literature particularly salient in its own arena of church social work practice.

The Content of this Book

This book provides an introduction to church social work, describing and illustrating practice principles that are particularly applicable in the varying contexts of church social work practice. The authors are all professional social workers who represent different denominations and levels of church organization, from local congregation to denominational and ecumenical agency.

Social workers often work with churches as part of their practice in any given American community, often from their places in a community's public and private social services agencies. Whether their role with churches is formalized or not, they serve in the role of a church social work consultant, helping the church to develop effective responses to community needs. The book begins with a description of church social work consultation. Derrell Watkins describes his own consultative relationship with a church which led to the development of a comprehensive family ministry program.

11

Increasingly, churches, particularly large congregations in urban areas, are employing social workers on their staffs to carry a number of responsibilities, from developing and directing the church's social ministries to providing counseling services for church and community members (Garland, 1987). In the third chapter, Jane Ferguson describes her work as the Director of Community Ministries on the staff of First Baptist Church, Montgomery, Alabama.

Many churches, however, have resources too limited to attempt to provide extensive social ministries on their own. By cooperating and pooling resources, churches of different denominations in the same community can employ professional staff and offer services designed specifically to meet the needs of their community. In the fourth chapter, Patricia Bailey describes the community ministry agency as a setting for social work practice.

One of the earliest formalized social ministries offered by churches was care of dependent children and youth. From these roots has sprung a whole array of services, including, for example, foster care and adoption, weekday early childhood education, and residential treatment facilities for emotionally disturbed youth. The church-related child welfare agency fills a prominent role in the array of child welfare services in American communities. In Chapter Five, I describe this setting for social work practice.

Social workers have been involved in the mission organizations of the church since the beginnings of the profession. Donoso Escobar, who himself directed the immigration and refugee service of one of the largest church mission organizations, The Southern Baptist Convention's Home Mission Board, describes social work practice in this context in Chapter Six.

Although churches have often been at the forefront of services to poor, oppressed, and marginalized persons and groups, they have been loudly silent at times when a prophetic voice was needed. Janet Spressart concludes the book by addressing the leadership church social work can provide churches in social action.

Conclusion

The church is a unique context for the practice of social work. Even though church social workers in settlement houses and community missions and centers share much in common with social workers in community outreach programs sponsored by public and private nonsectarian mental health and social service agencies, they work in a context with

12

subtle but nonetheless significant differences. The church's child welfare agency may offer foster and adoption services that look to the uninitiated much like the services of government and private nonsectarian agencies, but effective social work practice depends on sensitivity to the uniqueness of the church agency. We wrote this book to help church social workers define that uniqueness and develop those sensitivities to their practice context.

We believe that as important as it is for social workers to lead the church in social ministries, it is just as important that we provide a trail of where we have been and what we have learned bout that leadership, so that others can build on what we have learned and not repeat the mistakes we have made. To that end, we hope that this book will be another stone that marks the path of church social work, to be followed by many more that lead with greater certainty toward ever more effective church social work practice. Countless social workers have contributed to the development of church social work. In talking about science, Hans Zinsser (1990) noted that scientists build on their predecessors by choosing from all that they did what was the most significant. Thus, scientists select from the work of others the significant stepping stones that lead across difficulties to new understanding. The one who places the last stone and steps across to new land, establishing a path across the waters, gets all the credit. Yet that last step would not have been possible if it were not for the careful, devoted work of those who came before. In many respects, this book is simply a last stone that now defines a bridge. We have walked on the stones placed by many others; we have simply looked at the stones there, placed a final one, and called it a bridge--church social work. No doubt, others will come who will build a straighter, stronger bridge. With God's grace and Spirit, may this bridge be a clearer vision of who we are as church social workers, so that we can more effectively guide the church in ministry.

REFERENCES

Bailey, Patricia L. (1988). Southern Baptist programs of church social work. *Review and Expositor*, 85, 285-290.

Bau, Ignatius (1985). *This ground is holy: Church sanctuary and Central American refugees.* New York: Paulist Press.

Conrad, Anne P. (1980). Social ministry in the early church: An integral component of Christian community. *Social Thought,* 2, 41-51.

Davis, C. Anne (1983). The practice of urban ministry: Christian social ministries. *Review and Expositor*, 80, 523-536.

Davis, C. Anne (1988). History of the Carver School of Church Social Work. *Review and Expositor*, 85, 209-220.

Delamarter, Walter (1970). *The diakonic task*. Atlanta: Home Mission Board of the Southern Baptist Convention.

Edge, Findley B. (1983). Faith and mission: God's call to the laity. *Faith and Mission*, 1, 23.

Escobar, Donoso (1988). International church social work: A functional component in foreign missions. *Review and Expositor*, 85, 291-296.

Farnsworth, Kirk E. (1981). *Integrating psychology and theology: Elbows together but hearts apart*. Washington, D.C.: University Press of America.

Freeman, Margery (Ed.) (1986). *Called to act: Stories of child care advocacy in our churches*. Child Advocacy Office, Division of Church and Society, National Council of the Churches of Christ in the U.S.A., 475 Riverside Dr., Rm. 572, New York, NY 10115.

Garland, Diana R. (1985). Family life education, family ministry, and church social work: Suggested relationships. *Social Work and Christianity*, 12, 14-26.

Garland, Diana R. (1986). Christians in social work, Christian social ministry, and church social work: Necessary distinctions. *Social Work and Christianity*, 13, 18-25.

Garland, Diana R. (1987). Social workers on church staffs. Louisville: National Institute for Research and Training in Church Social Work.

Garland, Diana R. (1988). The church as a context for social work practice. *Review and Expositor*, 85, (2), 255-265.

Garland, Diana R. (submitted). The role of faith in practice with clients. *Social Work and Christianity*.

Garland, Diana R., and Bailey, Patricia L. (1990). Effective work with religious organizations by social workers in other settings. *Social Work and Christianity*, 17, 79-95.

Garland, Diana R., and Conrad, Ann P. (1990). The church as a context for professional practice. In Diana R. Garland and Diane L. Pancoast (Eds.) *The church's ministry with families*. Irving ,TX: Word.

Garland, D.S.R. (1987). *Social workers on church staffs*. Louisville: The National Institute for Research and Training in Church Social Work.

Garland, Diana R., and Pancoast, Diane L. (Eds.) (1990). *Churches ministering with families: A practical guide*. Irving, TX: Word.

Hessel, Dieter T. (1982). *Social ministry.* Philadelphia: Westminster Press.

Hinson, E. Glenn (1988). The historical involvement of the Church in social ministries and social action. *Review and Expositor,* 85, (2), 233-241.

Johnson, F. Ernest (1941). Protestant social work. In R.H. Kurtz (Eds.), *Social work year book.* New York: Russell Sage Foundation, pp. 403-412.

Johnson, Ronald, et al. (1977). *Social ministry manual.* Philadelphia: Parish Life Press.

Joseph, M.V., and Conrad, Anne P. (1988). *The parish as a ministering community: Social ministries in the local church community.* Hyattsville, MD: Pen Press.

Keith-Lucas, Alan (1960). Some notes on theology and social work. *Social Casework,* 41, 87-91.

Keith-Lucas, Alan (1972). *Giving and taking help.* Chapel Hill: University of North Carolina Press.

Keith-Lucas, Alan (1985). *So you want to be a social worker: A primer for the Christian student. S*t. Davids, PA: North American Association of Christians in Social Work.

Leonard, Bill J. (1988). The modern church and social action. *Review and Expositor,* 85, (2), 243-253.

Loewenberg, Frank M. (1988). *Religion and social work practice in contemporary American society.* New York: Columbia University Press.

Marty, Martin E. (1980). Social services: Godly and godless. *Social Service Review,* 54, 463-481.

Miles, Delos (1988). Church social work and evangelism: Partners in ministry. *Review and Expositor,* 85, 273-283.

Moberg, Daniel O. (1984). *The church as a social institution.* Grand Rapids: Baker Book House.

Morris, Robert (1986). *Rethinking social welfare: Why care for the stranger?* New York: Longman.

National Association of Social Workers (1985). *NASW data bank: Selected tables.* Silver Springs, MD: NASW. As cited in Loewenberg, 1988.

National Crime Prevention Council (1990). *Mission possible: Churches supporting fragile families.* Washington, D.C., National Crime Prevention Council.

Pinson, William M. (1971). *Applying the gospel: Suggestion for Christian social action in local church.* Nashville: Broadman Press.

Rainbow, Jon (1988). Social policy and church social work. *Review and Expositor,* 85, 267-272.

Smith, Timothy (1976). *Revivalism and social reform: American Protestantism on the eve of the Civil War*. Gloucester, MA: Peter Smith.

Spencer, Sue (1956). Religion and social work. *Social Work*, 1, 19-26.

Walker, T. Vaughn (1988). Luke 4:16-30. *Review and Expositor*, 85, 321-324.

Zinsser, Hans (1990). As quoted in Dicker, Sheryl, *Stepping stones: Successful advocacy for children*. NY: Foundation for Child development.

CHAPTER 2

Consultation in Church Social Work

by Derrel Watkins*

Social workers employed by church agencies often consult with congregations. A social worker on the staff of a community ministries agency consults with churches who want to start new ministries in the community such as tutoring and after school programs or self-help groups which address the needs and stressors of particular groups. She also works with churches in other communities who want to develop and support an ecumenical community ministry. Another social worker, employed by a residential child care facility, consults with churches in the state his agency serves. He helps them develop family services designed to prevent family problems that may result in out-of-home placement of children and youth.

Social workers in nonsectarian agencies also consult with churches to start needed programs. The One Church-One Child program was started by a social worker in a state child welfare agency. She became alarmed at the increasing number of African-American children waiting for adoption. She contacted an African-American priest and, in turn, pastors of other African-American congregations. Together, they developed a program which encourages and supports families who adopt children. The program has had significant effects, lowering the numbers of children waiting for adoption dramatically (Lakin & Hargett, 1986).

Consultation in church social work has much in common with mental health consultation. Primarily, social work and other mental health professions deal with *persons* in contradistinction to business management consultation that deals with products, productivity, profits, and losses. A bank, for example, must be concerned about the "bottom line" of investments and dividends. A mental health or church social service program is concerned about the quality of care given to a population of persons in need. The effectiveness of the social service program is measured by the number of persons served and the quality of that service. The goals and objectives of a church social service program will be stated in terms of the services planned and implemented and number of

*Derrel R. Watkins, Ed.D., ACSW, is Professor of Social Work, Southwestern Baptist Theological Seminary, Fort Worth, Texas.

17

persons to be reached by them.

Long before there were mental health or human service professions, the church was engaged in meeting the needs of human beings. The ministry of the church has been an expression of its concern for the "spiritual well-being" of persons inside and outside the community of faith. This quest for spiritual well-being has included concern for the physical, relational (social), emotional, mental, and the religious domains of living. It is almost impossible to separate spiritual wellness from these other domains. Neither can one be completely well if one does not possess a high level of spiritual well-being.

Consultation is not new to the church. Beginning with Genesis, one can see much evidence of advice from one outside the situation (the consultant) used by one experiencing difficulty (consultee). Exodus 18 records an organizational consultation. Moses' father-in-law, Jethro (the consultant), consulted with Moses (the consultee) regarding the organization of the tribes to increase the effectiveness and efficiency of the work. The prophets were consultants to leaders in Israel and Judah. When the nation heeded the consultation of the prophets, it prospered; when it did not, the nation suffered. For example, the result of King Ahaz's refusal to listen to Isaiah was the nation's defeat at the hands of the Assyrians (Isaiah 7). Later, when King Hezekiah heeded the prophet's advice, the Assyrians were defeated (Isaiah 36-39).

Much of the New Testament, especially the writings of Paul, are consultation reports to the early churches. Evidently, the churches sought advice from the apostle regarding many issues. Some of these were doctrine (II Timothy), ministry (Galatians 6), family problems (I Corinthians 6, 7), human relations (I Corinthians 13, Roman 12-14, Philemon, Galatians 3-4), economics (II Corinthians 9), and politics (Romans 13). Paul begins Chapter 7 of his first letter to the Corinthians acknowledging their questions. Apparently they had written to him regarding various sexual and other marital and family issues (I Corinthians 7:1-40).

The church social work *consultant* is a professional. The consultant has skill in the application of knowledge and skills in the delivery of services from a church context to individuals, families, groups, organizations and/or communities. The *consultee* is an individual or group of individuals working in a church, an agency, or organization in the community dealing with specialized needs of people (Beisser, 1972; Kadushin, 1977, Kelley, 1981).

Church program development relies on literature and consultation from the field of business management and organizational development. Most publications on church growth and church administration are adaptations of business management principles. These focus on organizational issues such as personnel enlistment and training, supervision and management, and time management for greater productivity and efficiency. This is translated into the number and size of Sunday School classes, plans for teacher and other leadership enlistment and training, evangelism and enlistment outreach, building and other space allocation, and budget promotion and management.

The specific contributions of mental health consultation, however, are more applicable for church social work. There are at least six common characteristics of this type of consultation (Parsons & Meyers, 1984).

First, it is a helping or problem-solving process. For example, if a church has identified a need in the community for day care for the children of parents who are working at or near minimum wages, the focus of consultation would be the description of the need for low-cost, quality child care; an assessment of the resources of both families in need of child care and the church; and the development of goals, objectives, and strategies for the provision of day care services under the auspices of the church.

Second, this consultation occurs with a consultee who has responsibility for the well-being of other persons. The church usually feels some responsibility for persons who are experiencing stress. Those parents who need quality day care for their children may represent to the pastor and staff of a congregation a group of persons whose well-being is in jeopardy.

Third, consultation is a voluntary relationship. The consultant is not imposed upon the church. The staff usually seeks out the consultant and the consultation agreement is engaged by mutual consent.

Fourth, the consultant and consultee share in solving the problem. The consultation process includes reliance upon the expertise of both the consultant and the consultee. That is, the pastor and staff are experts regarding the functioning of the congregation and usually have more familiarity with the community than the consultant does. The consultant is an expert on service delivery and program development. To develop an adequate day care program, there must be mutual respect for each other's areas of expertise and abilities.

Fifth, the goal of consultation is the resolution of a current work problem. The church staff is aware of the need for day care, but they probably do not have sufficient expertise for planning and implementing day care services. Therefore, the consultant works with the staff to resolve the problem created by the discrepancy between commitment to address a need and needed expertise.

Sixth, the consultee profits from the relationship so that future problems may be handled more skillfully. The obvious learning the staff may gain from this consultation is that the methodology used in the planning and delivery of day care services can be applied in the development of programs to meet other human needs. The staff may find that there are also families in the area who are providing care for their dependent older parents. They can apply the same process used in developing a day care program for children to the development of support programs for care-giving adult children.

Consultation may take the form of a one-day workshop. It may involve a one-time contact. It may extend over a period of weeks, months (or years), or it may extend indefinitely (Gallessich 1982; Caplan, 1970; Friedrich, 1990; Kadushin, 1977; Parsons & Meyers, 1984; Vacher, 1976).

The Need for Church Social Work Consultation

Many churches employ ministers who lead the congregation in the development and delivery of services to persons in need. Some ministers are professionally educated in social work, pastoral counseling or another mental health discipline. Some seminaries have specific education programs for church social workers. One seminary grants the Master of Social Work degree.[1] Other seminaries have social work training in their curricula or enter into cooperative relationships with nearby graduate schools of social work to provide specific training in this field.

These seminaries do not represent the majority, however. Even where the training is available, only small minorities of seminarians take advantage of it. This suggests a need for consultants, especially for those churches with social ministries or those who want to develop such ministries for which the clergy cannot provide the needed leadership. Even when the church leader has the needed education, the church may require the services of an outside consultant to help in the development or improvement of programming and the quality of services delivered by the church.

Church social work consultants may work with ministers or congregation in a variety of settings. For example, an outside consultant with expertise in the development of inner-city ministries may be of service to churches in changing neighborhoods in both urban and suburban settings. As gentrification takes place in the downtown areas of some cities

---

1 The Carver School of Church Social Work of The Southern Baptist Theological Seminary, Louisville, Kentucky.

inner-city residents move to older suburban communities. These suburban neighborhoods face fewer owner-occupied homes, similar to the inner-city. With this phenomenon comes an increase in crime, drug and alcohol abuse, teen-age gangs, prostitution, property deterioration, and a general loss of community pride. A church social worker, trained in community intervention, may provide expert advice regarding the process of networking with formal and informal systems in the community. Developing programs of ministry outreach to specific populations at risk is also a part of this expertise.

As the world grows smaller through the increased use of rapid transportation and sophisticated communication technology, most congregations discover that they are located in multi-cultural communities. Traditional ministries may not meet the needs of these new citizens/immigrants/refugees. A church social work consultant who has training and expertise in cross-cultural service delivery may be very valuable to such congregations. For example, the consultant may help the ministries or missions committee of the congregation to understand the differences and commonalities of the new residents in the community with one another and with the congregation. The consultant can then lead the committee to develop culturally sensitive programs of service that acknowledge the new residents' uniqueness and include them as members of the community.

A Model for Church Social Work Consultation

Although there have been some publications regarding social work consultation as far back as 1936, the general field of mental health has provided the most significant models.[2] In his classic work, *The Theory and Practice of Mental Health Consultation*, Gerald Caplan (1970) suggested four consultation types that will form the basis of the model suggested here for church social work consultation. They are: (1) client-centered case consultation; (2) consultee-centered case consultation; (3) program-centered administrative consultation; and (4) consultee-centered administrative consultation.

---

2 One of the earliest publications about consultation in social work practice was an article entitled "The Use of a Consultation Method in Casework Therapy" by Sloane, 1936. Two papers were presented to the American Association of Medical Social Workers in New Orleans, published in 1942. Papers on consultation from the 1954 Social Welfare Forum were Client-Centered Case Consultation published by the Family Service Association in 1955. The Hogg Foundation for Mental Health published a book entitled The Case Work Consultant and Visiting Nurses by Rader and Whidden, 1960. Lydia Rapoport's classic work, Consultation in Social Work Practice, was published by the National Association of Social Workers in 1963.

A church social worker is working with an alcoholic family where the father is addicted and the other family members are co-dependent. They have come to the church social worker for help in breaking their co-dependency and want help with counseling and intervening with the addict. The church social worker, however, is not experienced in holding family intervention sessions with alcoholics. The worker feels that she is "stuck" and, in the best interest of the client system, seeks consultation from a social worker in an alcohol and drug treatment facility who has experience in family treatment. The consultant meets with the client system and makes recommendations regarding strategies of intervention. That is "client-centered case consultation." The focus is on the needs of the client and possible strategies of intervention which will deal effectively with those needs (Kadushin, 1977).

This type of consultation is basic to the process of professional supervision. However, there are some circumstances where the consultant will be asked to continue the treatment. If, in the example above, the church social worker was not comfortable in mediating a family intervention with the alcoholic father, the consultant may be asked to take charge of the case and supervise the intervention. The family would either continue to see the church social worker for counseling after the intervention or the consultant would be asked to take ongoing case responsibility, and a referral takes place from consultee to consultant.

Consultee-Centered Case Consultation

If, in the situations mentioned above, the consultee calls upon the consultant to assess the methods and techniques used by the consultee, the focus of the consultation would be consultee-centered. Emphasis is not upon the client but upon the consultee's skills in working with a particular client or group of clients (Kadushin, 1977; Mannino, et. al, 1975). This type of consultation is also used in professional supervision.

Professional organizations such as the National Association of Social Workers (NASW) usually require professional supervision of a worker's practice in order to qualify for membership in the Academy of Certified Social Workers (ACSW). The American Association for Marriage and Family Therapy (AAFMT) requires a similar process for clinical membership. A portion of this supervision may be included in the worker's formal graduate education, but a significant part must be acquired while on the job. States with laws regulating counseling, marriage and family therapy and/or other forms of social work normally require at least 2,000 hours of practice under the supervision of an approved professional supervisor. Similar to the standards for membership in professional organizations, state licensing/certification regulations usually require that most of these hours be acquired after receiving an approved terminal degree such as the Master of Social Work or the Ph.D. in Psychology. This type of supervision is often received from a consultant outside the organization. The consultant will be asked to read case histories, observe video tapes, observe the therapist in action, and discuss all the cases with the worker.

In church social work, consultee-centered case consultation can be particularly helpful to the consultee dealing with the complex issues of a church setting. For example, the consultant may help the consultee process issues concerning professional practice with church members with whom the consultee serves on church committees, or issues of confidentiality or conflicting values and ethical stances.

Program-Centered Administrative Consultation

Most consultations sought by churches are about specific issues in programming. Specialists study the church's target population, constituency of the congregation, and available resources (human and economic). For example, a church is located in a neighborhood that has been totally surrounded by a major university with its dormitories, apartments for student, faculty and other staff families, and classroom buildings. The leadership of the church feels unprepared to reach out to the community and minister to the unique needs of this population. A church social work consultant may be engaged to help the church assess the spiritual, physical, emotional, and relational needs of the university community and to develop short and long range plans for social service programs designed to meet these needs (Hasenfeld & English, 1974; Neugeboren, 1985; Tripodi, et. al., 1978; Peters, 1987).

Skills in organizational development and program evaluation will be used by the consultant in this type of consultation (Tripodi, et. al., 1978; Litterer, 1973; Grinnell, 1981; Attkisson, et. al., 1978; Austin, et. al., 1982). In the example above, the church social work consultant would encourage the church to examine its mission (purpose) statement (or write one if none exists), its goals, history, self-concept, style of organization and administration, worship style, policies regarding the utilization of church buildings and property, schedules, and ethical and normative parameters (i.e., dress codes, social activities, etc.). Questions such as: Is the Mission Statement still valid? Do the goals encompass the needs of the new population? Are the church's organizational structure and administrative policies flexible enough to accommodate the unique demands this new population will make upon it? How much change in the worship style can the congregation tolerate? Will other styles of music and worship be tolerated? Will the congregation be open to variations of schedules for worship and religious education? Are there "untouchable" areas of the buildings and grounds that the congregation will refuse to modify, if necessary, in order to minister to this new population? Can the schedule accommodate using buildings and property at varying times of the day and night? What about dress codes, i.e., if community residents show up for worship in slacks, jeans, shorts, or sweats, will they be welcomed? Will they feel conspicuous? Are goals and objectives written in behaviorally specific terms so that they may be measured concretely? Is the church willing to commit the financial and personnel resources necessary for such a ministry? What measures of effectiveness will be important for changes and additions in programs and activities?

Consultee-Centered Administrative Consultation

There may be times in a congregation's life when programs develop problems or are not meeting their objectives. A consultant can help the staff study the various aspects of its administration (Attkisson, et. al., 1978; Austin, et. al., 1982). The consultant does not necessarily give attention to such issues as population statistics or organizational mission. Instead, the consultant directs attention toward the study of issues such as leadership style, resource acquisition and allocation, outreach methods, public relations, scheduling, group dynamics, interpersonal relationship skills, staff conflict resolution, and supervision (Mannino, et. al., 1975; Kadushin, 1977; Kelley, 1981; Ginzberg & Reilley, 1966; Beisser, 1972). Let's suppose, in the example of the church surrounded by the university community, the ministers became concerned that very few students, faculty, and staff were taking advantage of the worship, religious education, and other ministries offered by the church. The church social work consultant might help them to discover the reason(s) the community was not responding. It might be that the preaching style, the music, or the teaching style in the Bible classes may not meet the needs of these community groups. Volunteers working in the ministry programs may have problematic attitudes. Schedules of services may not be convenient. The university community may not be aware of the services, or the services may not be targeting a perceived need. The consultant would help the consultee to discover the cause of ineffectiveness and make needed changes.

Most congregations tend to use inside consultants. An inside consultant is a knowledgeable person who, working within the congregation, studies a situation and makes recommendations regarding changes in the congregation's programming or service delivery process. The insider, or "in-house" consultant, has the advantage of knowing more about the church, agency, or judicatory, understanding the context, background and resources, and possessing in-depth knowledge and continuity of experience with the church, agency, or judicatory (Gallessich, 1982). Church social workers on the staff of regional judicatories may, by definition, serve as consultants to all the constituent congregations in their areas. Their job is to respond to requests from congregations or ministers for consultation regarding various aspects of church social service planning and delivery.

There are some disadvantages to using an in-house consultant. One, since the church, agency, or judicatory may be providing the income for the consultants, consultants may be tempted to be more cautious. Two, touchy issues may be avoided because they are threatening both to the consultants and to the consultee. Three, consultants are attempting to be "prophets in their own land" and may find it difficult to legitimize the consultation. Four, even if they accept the inside consultant's consultation, other staff members tend to attribute greater expertise to outsiders. Five, hierarchical status is a sensitive issue, since persons of higher rank tend to discount the expertise of one who is of lower rank. For example, a pastor may feel that his expertise in church-related or theological issues is superior to that of a church social work consultant and thus discount any new information gained through the consultation. Six, objectivity may be difficult for the consultant and the consultee. Seven, consultants and consultees may have a dual relationship that could involve role conflicts (Gallessich, 1982). For example, the consultee may be the chairperson of the personnel committee which supervises the consultant as an employee.

Consultants who are financially, socially, and emotionally independent of the consultee system can more easily take risks, such as challenging traditions, asking "obvious" questions that no one has considered posing before, or suggesting personnel and policy changes that may be threatening to a member of the staff or congregation. Their temporary relationship allows either the church or the consultant to terminate if adverse conditions should arise such as when a consultant has suggested significant changes that engender hostility in the staff, resulting in a lack of cooperation. Finally, the consultee almost inevitably values the contributions of a paid consultant more than those who are available free of charge (Gallessich, 1982).

There are situations that call for expertise from outside the congregation. Church social work consultants may prove invaluable when congregations undertake ministry programs with persons who are experiencing various personal and family crises, such as family life stage transitions, divorce adjustment, substance abuse and other addictions in self or family members, family violence, sexual abuse, imprisonment, illness, rape, suicide of a family member, and issues associated with various forms of mental illness. The church social work consultant could refer church leaders to training materials, assist in training lay leaders, train support group leaders, and assist churches to develop other strategies for reaching and ministering to these persons and families.

Phases in the Church Social Work Consultation Process

Lippitt and Lippitt (1978) identify six phases in the consulting process; contact and entry; formulating a contract and establishing a helping relationship; problem identification and diagnostic analysis; goal setting and planning; taking action and cycling feedback; and contract completion (continuity, support and termination). These phases are generic in the helping process.

The pastor and the leaders of a congregation sought the consultation of the Director of Christian Social Ministries for a local association of churches. The congregation's regular ministry programs did not appear to be making a significant difference in the lives of families and adolescents in the immediate neighborhood. Family violence was increasing. Substance abuse appeared to be the norm among a large segment of adolescents and young adults in the neighborhood. Many of these had once been a part of the church's day-care and day-school education ministry and Sunday school programs. They determined that an outside consultant would be employed to give guidance to the development of a program of family intervention.

Making Initial Contact

Whether the consultant is a specialist in direct services, as in client-centered cased consultation and consultee-centered case consultation, or an administration and planning specialist, as in program-centered administrative consultation or consultee-centered administrative consultation, entry into the consultation relationship is crucial. Although they have not formally identified themselves as professional consultants, many are drawn into the consultation role by requests from friends and others who call upon them for assistance. Often they begin as in-house consultants by assisting co-workers with individual cases or with problems in

26

planning, programming, or supervision. Others enter the field of mental health consultation as a vocation after gaining training and experience (Beisser, 1972; Caplan, 1970; Kadushin, 1977; Kelley, 1981; Mannino, et. al., 1975; Parsons & Meyers, 1984; Vacher, 1976).

Ideally, the potential consultee makes the first move toward employing a consultant. The consultee, recognizing a need, makes the initial contact and arranges to discuss the situation. The consultant identifies and clarifies the need for change in the consultee's situation. The next task is to determine the readiness of the consultee or the consultee's congregation for change (Beisser 1972). During this exploratory period, the prospective consultant and consultee decide if they have the potential for a productive consultation.

The pastor of the inner-city church contacted the Home Mission Board of his denomination. He was put in touch with a church social work consultant, who agreed to serve as a consultant to the church for six to ten months.

Formulating a Professional Relationship and Developing a Contract

Even if the consultant is a friend or co-worker, the relationship needs to be formalized in order to be effective; that is, an agreement defining the parameters of the consultation should be stipulated. Both the consultant and consultee must have a clear idea of what is to be achieved because of this relationship. Questions such as the following must be answered: Who is to do what, when, how, and under whose initiative? What data, financial resources, equipment, space, and personnel will be involved or at the disposal of the consultant? To whom will the consultant report?

A contract can be an informal, verbal agreement between the parties involved. Experience has taught, however, that it is more desirable to put the specific answers to the above questions in a written contract. The consultant may draft a written agreement or the consultee may draft it, but both must be in agreement before it will be effective (Beisser, 1972; Caplan, 1970; Gallessich, 1982; Kadushin, 1977; Parsons & Meyers, 1984).

An initial contract was developed. The congregation would provide temporary office space, office supplies, stationary, secretarial assistance, a telephone line (which would later become the telephone number for the program developed out of the consultant's work), mailing expenses, a filing cabinet, and a typewriter. The consultant would have access to all the congregation records and serve as an adjunct staff member, attending all staff functions.

The congregation, with the local judicatory, would provide the financial resources, including travel expenses, for the consultation.

The consultant would study the needs of the congregation and community and make regular reports to the congregation and the judicatory. An advisory committee would be appointed by the pastor and members of the church staff and the judicatory would participate in committee meetings as ex-officio members. All members of the committee would help the consultant in gathering information and providing feedback regarding the various aspects of the congregation, pertinent to the type of ministry being developed.

The congregation, with the assistance of the judicatory, would be responsible for deciding whether to adopt and implement any recommendations from the consultation.

The consultant, after meeting with the church staff and the appointed committee, drafted a preliminary contract that specified each element of the contract. It stated what the congregation, staff, and judicatory would do. It also specified what the function of the consultant would be regarding all elements of the consultation. This was presented to the advisory committee, who then refined and presented it to the congregation for approval.

Problem Identification and Analysis

Peter Gaupp, a social work professor at the University of Texas at Arlington, states that it is just as important to know your enemies and what the basis of their objections are likely to be as it is to know what you want to do and who will support you in doing it. Lippitt and Lippitt (1978, p. 17) refer to this process as "force-field diagnosis." The forces and counterforces at work within each client system need to be identified and addressed in the consultation. For example, in this case it was important to know if there were any congregational leaders who were resistant to the development of a family ministry. If so, what was the nature of their objections? How strong was their influence over the decision making process of the congregation? Was it possible to convince them to support the development of the ministry?

Problem identification must begin by gathering appropriate information about the client system. This includes: (1) the level of functioning in each domain of living (spiritual, physical, mental, emotional, relational, and economic); and (2) the possible causes of any dysfunction (personal limitations, environmental deficiencies, rules, regulations, practices, or a crisis or catastrophe). In addition, the consultant should work with the consultee to determine what the client system is already doing to resolve the problem, how well the intervention is working, and why what is being done is not producing the desired outcome (Attkisson, et. al., 1978; Austin, et. al., 1982; Bloom & Fischer, 1982; Fine & Wiley, 1971; Grinnell, 1981; Litterer, 1973; Neugeboren, 1985; Tripodi, et. al., 1978).

The first action of the consultant was to gather information regarding the various social problems that existed within the immediate neighborhood. He discovered that there had been a recent study of the needs of the community that gave specific data regarding all the concerns that had originally been suggested by the pastor. He contacted community social service agencies to gather additional, more up-to-date data and attitudes regarding these problems. Since the development of a new service delivery system may be perceived as threatening by some service providers, he wanted to determine the level of support or objection each would have for the church's proposed family ministry program. He found that there was general support, but there was a surplus of psychologists and other counselors in the community and the addition of another program could be perceived as additional competition for mental health resources (fees and insurance payments).

He discovered that alcoholism and other substance abuse was a major problem, well above the national average. Divorce and other forms of family dysfunction were either at or above the national average. The incidence of family violence was alarmingly higher than the national average for communities of this size. Although the community was multi-cultural, these problems did not appear to be concentrated in one ethnic group but disseminated throughout the community.

A study of the congregation revealed a concern for family dysfunction among family members related to the membership. They also expressed concern for the dysfunctional families in the community. Median and older adults were more concerned about marital strife and divorce, while younger adults were concerned about husband-wife relationships and parenting skills. There was a significant concern expressed regarding single parenting.

The consultant found that persons in the community were significantly unconcerned about spiritual issues. This was particularly true among mental health service providers. The percentage who attended worship services of any religion was significantly below the national average. Incidence of mental illness was close to the national average. The literacy level was slightly above average. Although the cost of living was significantly above the national average, the income level was slightly below average. Adequate, affordable housing was difficult to find. The divorce rate was slightly above the national average.

The church was already providing several programs that were dealing with some of the community's needs. An emergency food and clothing program was functioning very well. A local association operated a literacy and job-training program in the church building. Divorce adjustment and support groups met in the church facilities under the leadership of a local organization. The church's day care and pre-school program had an excellent community service reputation.

Intervention Strategy Planning

After gathering and studying demographic and other information, the consultant and consultee together revise the goals of the intervention or formulate new goals and objectives. These goals and objectives should be stated in behavioral terminology, using action verbs and specific outcomes such as, "In order to provide affordable family services the center will acquire funding, of sufficient amount, to underwrite the salaries of the church social worker and the support staff, thereby relieving the center of the burden of depending upon client fees to sustain its staff." Goals and objectives should be measurable; that is, their achievement (or lack of achievement) should be obvious. For example, this goal is measurable in that when funding is arranged, of sufficient amounts to cover the salaries of the social worker and support staff, it will have been reached. Fees charged to clients will not be crucial to the operation of the program and, therefore, can be assessed at a level the client can afford.

Goals and objectives lead to the development of specific action strategies that will be used to achieve them. These strategies state (1) what is to be done, (2) when it is to be done, (3) by whom it is to be done, (4) how it is to be done, (5) where the action will take place, (6) what resources (economic and human) will be used, and (7) what instructions/procedures will be followed under whose direct supervision (Fine & Wiley, 1971).

A mission statement was drafted. Goals and objectives were written. Action strategies were developed, including a chart delineating the steps to be taken at specific times by specific persons. This included acquiring, allocating, and using specific resources as the program developed. Job descriptions were written that specified the specific functions, responsibilities, and supervisory relationships of each position. This report was presented to the congregation for formal approval.

The consultant, working with the committee and staff, identified specific areas of concern that could be addressed, using the congregation's resources. These included three levels of programming: (1) enrichment, i.e., programs designed to strengthen existing healthy family systems in the congregation and community. (2) prevention, i.e., anticipating potential family dysfunctions, providing education such as short term training in family communication and problem solving, family finances, etc., and activities such as couple retreats, senior adult retreats, youth retreats, and family retreats; and (3) treatment, i.e., make counseling services available for dysfunctional individuals, families, and groups.

Taking Action and Providing Feedback

Consultation does not end with the development of plans and action strategies. These must be implemented and evaluated at predetermined points in the process. The consultant is not responsible for implementing the plans. As the plans are implemented, however, the consultant monitors them and provides feedback to the consultee regarding the effectiveness and efficiency of the intervention or program (Tripodi, et. al., 1978).

Recommendations for modifications are made by the consultant. These include suggestions for revising action plans and mobilizing additional resources. The consultee is then responsible for their implementation. The consultant remains available and continues to monitor the progress of the intervention.

The Family Ministry Program enlisted a social worker, who was a member of the church, to be the director. Another member, a clinical psychologist, became a part-time director of counseling. The program offered parenting classes, a young-adult couples retreat, a class on relationships between adult children and their aging parents, a congregation-wide family enrichment weekend, a single adult support group, and a single-adult parenting class. An adult-child-of-dysfunctional families support group began as a result of the interest of several clients in the counseling program.

After each event, the consultant analyzed the project and made recommendations for future programs. The consultant continued to meet with the committee. He also continued to train and supervise the Family Ministry Program staff. Additional social workers, pastoral counselors, and psychologists were enlisted to provide counseling services and lead in educational programs. Some of these were members of the congregation and some were members of other churches in the community. Referral relationships were developed with other social service and mental health providers in the community.

Analysis of the client population in the initial phase of the program revealed that 30 percent came from the congregation; 40 percent were Christians, referred by other congregations; and 30 percent were non-Christians who were self-referred or referred by staff members of other agencies or churches.

Termination and Evaluation

One step taken in the termination of a consultation is the development of a continuing support plan. That is, how will the consultee make additional use of the consultant if a need arises in the future? If the consultant will no longer be available to the church, this should be clearly stated. If the consultant is going to be available on a contingency basis, however, the conditions for such an arrangement should be made, in writing if possible.

Client-centered case consultation will normally be terminated after a short period of time, with the door left open for additional consultation if the need arises. Other cases may replace the one that has been the focus of the consultation. The contract for this type of consultation should be specifically stated and agreed to by both the consultant and the consultee.

Administrative and program centered consultation implies a different type of termination. An insider should be trained to carry out the tasks the consultant performed. i.e., monitoring and evaluating the progress of the program or organization.

Normally the consultation will be phased out gradually, according to a predetermined set of guidelines. The consultee gradually reduces the budget, as previously scheduled. The consultee considers including other outside helpers from time to time. The consultant produces a final report that documents the process and results of the consultation. The consultee may plan a celebration, where the consultant presents the final report. Together, consultee and consultant develop a maintenance plan with, perhaps, an annual review session.

After nine months, the consultation was terminated. Local, in-house consultants were enlisted to continue the project. The consultant made a final report to the congregation and developed an operations manual for the center.

Conclusion

Most churches do not have the resources to employ a church social worker on their staff. Yet they find themselves located in the heart of communities experiencing overwhelming social problems and visiting in the living rooms of families frightened by or actually suffering the effects of those problems. Often, these families are members of the congregation. Many churches want to help; they see ministry to suffering persons and families to be at the heart of their very reason for existence. Church social workers, through consultation, can help them capture a vision of what they can do to help, can help them assess their resources of money and facilities and volunteers and calling, and can help them gain the knowledge and skills they need to care in effective ways in Jesus' name.

REFERENCES

American Association of Medical Social Workers (1942). *Consultation.* Menasha, Wisconsin: George Banta Publishing Company.

Attkisson, G. Clifford; Hargreaves, William A.; Horowitz, Mardi J.; and Sorensen, James E. (1978). *Evaluation of human service programs.* New York: Academic Press.

Austin, Michael J., Cox, Gary; Gottlieb, Naomi; Hawkins, J. David; Kruzich, Jean M;, and Rauch, Ronald (1982). *Evaluating your agency's programs.* Beverly Hills: Sage Publications.

Beisser, Arnold (1972). *Mental health consultation and education.* Palo Alto, CA: National Press Books.

Bennis, Warren G.; Benne, Kenneth D.; Chin, Robert; and Corey, Kenneth E. (1976). *The planning of change.* (3rd Ed.) New York: Holt, Rinehart and Winston.

Bloom, Martin and Fischer, Joel (1982). *Evaluating practice: Guidelines for the accountable professional.* Englewood Cliffs: Prentice-Hall, Inc.

Caplan, Gerald (1970). *The theory and practice of mental health consultation.* New York and London: Basic Books, Inc., Publishers.

Fine, Sidney and Wiley, Wretha (1971). *An introduction to functional job analysis.* Kalamazoo, MI: The W.E. Upjohn Institute for Employment Research.

Friedrich, Laura Dean (1990). Serving children and families through agency consultation. In D. Garland and D. Pancoast (Eds.), *The church's ministry with families: A practical guide.* Irving, TX: Word, pp. 155-170.

Gallessich, June (1982). *The profession and practice of consultation.* San Francisco: Jossey-Bass Publishers.

Ginzberg, Eli and Reilley, Ewing (1966). *Effective change in large organizations.* New York and London: Columbia University Press.

Grinnell, Richard M. (Ed.) (1981). *Social work research and evaluation.* Itasca, IL: F.E. Peacock Publishers, Inc.

Hasenfeld, Yeheskil and English, Richard A. (Eds.) (1974). *Human service organizations.* Ann Arbor: The University of Michigan Press.

Kadushin, Alfred (1977). *Consultation in social work.* New York: Columbia University Press.

Kelley, Robert E. (1981). *Consulting.* New York: Charles Scribner's Sons.

Lakin, Drenda, and Hargett, J. (1986). The role of the Black Church in the adoption of black children with developmental disabilities. Paper presented to the NASW Clinical Social Work Conference, San Francisco, September 12, 1986.

Lippitt, Gordon and Lippitt, Ronald (1978). *The consulting process in action.* La Jolla, CA: University Associates, Inc.

Litterer, Joseph A. (1973). *The analysis of organizations.* New York: John Wiley & Sons, Inc.

Mannino, Fortune V., MacLennan, B.W. and Shore, M.F. (Eds.) (1975). *The practice of mental health consultation.* New York: Gardner Press, Inc.

National Conference on Social Work (1955). *Administration, supervision, and consultation.* New York: Family Service Association of America.

Neugeboren, Bernard (1985). *Organization, policy, and practice in the human services.* New York and London: Longman.

Parsons,, Richard D., and Meyers, Joel (1984). *Developing consultation skills.* San Francisco: Jossey-Bass Publishers.

Peters, Tom (1987). *Thriving on chaos.* New York: Harper & Row, Publishers.

Rader, M.T., and Whidden, A.G. (1960). *The case work consultant and visiting nurses.* Austin, TX: The Hogg Foundation for Mental Health.

Sloane, P. (1936). The use of a consultation method in casework therapy. *American Journal of Orthopsychiatry,,* 6, 2, 355-361.

Tripodi, Tony, Fellin, Phillip, and Epstein, Irwin. (1978). *Differential social program evaluation.* Itasca, IL: F.E. Peacock Publishers, Inc.

Vacher, Carole D. (1976). *Consultation-education development and evaluation.* New York: Human Sciences Press.

CHAPTER 3

The Congregation as Context for Social Work Practice

*by Jane Ferguson**

Christian social ministries can be the caring connection between the local church and the community. Caring love builds bridges. God calls the church to relate redemptively to those in need within and outside the local church. Many churches find themselves nestled in or near the declining areas of the inner city, unable to ignore easily the poverty, unemployment, crowded conditions, powerlessness, abuse and ill health of these city dwellers. Churches also find themselves faced with the plight of many ethnic groups, Native Americans, and persons with special emotional or physical needs who live on the margins of society. Active caring embodies to these persons and groups the gospel the church teaches and preaches.

In 1985, believing that the church must address the needs of the whole person physically, emotionally, socially, and spiritually, L. Dale Huff, pastor of First Baptist Church of Montgomery, Alabama, began to dream of such a program for his congregation. How could he lead his people to become more involved in the lives of hurting people? How could he move this congregation of 2000 into a more proactive ministry that addressed the needs of its neighbors, the surrounding community? By examining the experiences of this church as they employed a social worker to lead them in Christian social ministry, this chapter explores the role of the social worker on a congregational staff.

Every church has its own history which gives shape to its present concerns and ministry. Effective church leaders learn and build on a church's history and understanding of itself. First Baptist Church, Montgomery, Alabama, has a one hundred and sixty year history of innovative ministry; it is located three blocks from downtown Dexter Avenue, birthplace of the Black civil rights movement. From the church's earliest beginnings, local, state and foreign missions have been top priorities. First Baptist has been home for many denominational leaders, college presidents, and

---

*Jane Ferguson, MSW, is Director of Community Ministries, First Baptist Church, Montgomery, Alabama.

community leaders. Included in its membership have been three state governors along with mayors, state educators, military personnel from the nearby Air Force base, and Alabama Supreme Court justices. One such prominent Montgomerian is U.S. District Judge Frank M. Johnson, Jr., know for his civil rights rulings of the 1960s. Perhaps this church is known most for its strong pastoral leadership, its generosity, and its enviable record of lay participation. In 1990, the total church budget was $1,825,000. Approximately $195,000 was designated for mission causes.

In 1985, First Baptist made the intentional decision to remain in downtown Montgomery. The church knew remaining downtown meant doing more to address the problems related to the poverty of its neighboring community. Simply staying in the community was not enough. Under the direction of the pastor, the Long Range Planning Committee determined that there was a need for a special ministry to help the church carry out its biblical mandate to be good stewards of the church's resources. A commitment was made to hire an additional ministerial staff person to develop this program. The church hired its first social worker to be employed on the staff of a Southern Baptist church in the state of Alabama.

Characteristics of Church Social Work with a Congregation

Three characteristics distinguish social work on the staff of a congregation from the practice of social work in other settings: the context of the local church, the professional identity of the social worker, and the focus of practice.

First, the context of the local church provides a natural state for reaching some groups who may be hard to reach for other agencies and social institutions. Most people understand the church and its role in their lives. Especially in the Bible belt of the South, the church is a place to go in time of trouble. Ann, an African-American college student distraught over a personal crisis, wandered into First Baptist looking for a minister with whom to talk. The church receptionist called for the church social worker. The young woman was suicidal and wanted to know what God would do when she took her life that day. The social worker's assurance of God's loving concern aided in her acceptance of treatment. During the most critical time of her life, she had turned to the church for help.

The church social worker usually has the opportunities for an ongoing role in the natural network of relationships of community residents. Social work practice is thus less formal than in many other practice settings, woven as it is into neighborhood and congregational activities. In contrast, most non-church related social service agencies are task centered, focusing on relationship only as they function to accomplish specified goals for the agency.

Since the church and its language and rituals are woven into the fabric of community life, words like "sin," "salvation," and "forgiveness," are familiar terms. It often becomes the responsibility of the church social worker to interpret life events in biblical language that the client understands and appreciates.

Janet Dunn is a very religious woman going through a divorce. She is overwhelmed with guilt and shame, believing that divorce is a terrible sin. Despite the fact that she and her children have been emotionally and sexually abused, she is confused about how this divorce will effect her relationship with God. Janet will find comfort and support in being assured by a respected representative of the church that God is a loving God who does not condone abuse.

The opposite can also be true, however. Clients can be alienated or confused by church language, however well intended. The church social worker must be aware that often there is much work to be done before a person can even begin to comprehend the love of God. Therefore, the gospel must be acted out in tangible ways--as the church provides funds for a family in financial crisis or friendship to persons feeling isolated and alone.

The second distinction for social work in a local church is the church social worker's professional identity and calling as a minister. The church social worker accepts the challenge of combining knowledge base, skills and values of both social work and professional ministry. A church social worker often is seen by the client as God's representative.

Third, the church social worker's focus of practice in a congregation is broader than practice in many other settings, including preventive, rehabilitative, and proactive--as well as reactive--responses to a variety of human needs. The social worker embodies God's care for the whole person. The social worker does not use ministry programs as bait to do evangelism, but instead provides the congregation with alternatives for living out the Good News. According to Kenneth Chafin, "Evangelism moves best on the wings of ministry" (1988).

Integrating Faith and Practice

One of the most personal challenges for the social worker on a congregational staff is the integration of religious mission with the practice of social work. The social worker on a congregational staff must communicate to the professional social work community a commitment to uphold the standards of the profession; the church social worker often becomes suspect by the social work profession of wanting to proselytize rather than help, of wishing to impose his or her beliefs on others, of being rigid and judgmental or rejecting the findings of science when they appear to conflict with dogma (Keith-Lucas, 1956). Proving one's self as a peer in the social work profession begins from the outset of the contact stage.

The social worker at First Baptist Montgomery has had to work extremely hard not to be seen by the professional community as a moral arbiter but a professional who models love, forgiveness and care. Often it is necessary for the church social worker to confront the religious stereotypes held by many professionals in the community. Upholding the standards of the social work profession frequently brings verbal or nonverbal responses of surprise from community leaders.

To be successful in the local church, the church social worker must develop a program based on sound biblical and theological principles, the value foundation of the church. Building community ministries on biblical teaching provides the church with impetus for ministry. Jesus ate with publicans and sinners. Jesus talked to the Samaritan woman at the well. Therefore, we are to have an attitude of respect and openness toward persons with different lifestyles.

First Baptist Church volunteers, with the church social worker's guidance, work with HIV positive patients at Julia Tutwiler Women's Prison. Faye, a former drug user, had a "crack" baby dying of AIDS. The social worker provided counseling and coordinated her work with the services of Montgomery AIDS Outreach, a community based agency. Volunteers provide friendship and spiritual counseling and support. Although the social worker and volunteers do not agree with some of the lifestyle choices Faye has made, they embody God's care for her and for her child.

The social worker emphasizes her professional social work identity in the secular community and her role as minister/clergy in the religious setting, translating social work language into religious language and vice versa. The church social worker is often called upon to make clear her position both to the congregation and the community. First Baptist Church has many church members who had no idea what a social worker does; the social worker has had to carve out and describe her role for them. Similarly, since no one in the community had ever met a social worker who is part of a congregation's ministerial staff, they often ask if the social worker is a volunteer or if her husband is a minister. If social workers are not clear in their own mind who they are, these questions can create identity confusion. Earning the respect of the helping community is accomplished through exemplary professionalism both as a social worker and as clergy.

A Biblical and Theological Basis for Local Church Social Work

One of the most difficult tasks of the social worker on a local church staff is to confront and dismantle the myths in many congregations surrounding the poor and disenfranchised of our society. To meet this challenge, one must have a sound biblical and theological foundation as well as an understanding of the social sciences. Building a redemptive and caring community of faith requires ongoing cooperation and concerted effort from the entire ministerial staff. Shaping the consciousness of the congregation is a ministry within itself; not only do people have to be taught how to care, but they need to be equipped with a basis for caring. The church social worker must model, through both words and deeds, a positive, nonjudgmental attitude toward the poor and others who may be the focus of stereotypes by church members and staff.

First Baptist Church has many people who walk in off the street seeking assistance. When the social worker joined the staff, many staff members were indignant with these people, and often made derogatory jokes and sarcastic remarks. Without commenting on staff attitudes, the social worker modeled love and respect for these people. The negative remarks disappeared.

The early Christians focused on the needs of people without questioning whether they were worthy or unworthy. Sadly, the modern day church sometimes emphasizes helping only the "deserving" person. Many church members view economic success as God's favor and work as a product of faith. Capitalism and the Protestant work ethic often take precedence in ideology over biblical teaching.

The theological framework for social work practice in First Baptist Church began with the radical imperative that Christians reflect their love for God through loving neighbors as self, and with the mandate to seek justice and peace. This requires Christians to deal with problems of public life and with the structures, policies, and institutions of society that oppress. The theme of solidarity with victims runs throughout the entire Bible, from early Old Testament (Exodus 22:21-22) to late New Testament (James 1:22-27). When the Bible deals with justice, it tends to be very specific, naming such groups as widows and orphans, poor people, and strangers. The Old Testament prophets pronounced judgment upon those who oppressed or turned aside from doing justice, who robbed the poor of their rights and took spoil from the widows, and who made the fatherless their prey (Isaiah 10:1-2). The Old Testament prophets also summoned the people to "do justice" as a response to what their God had done for them, calling them to act as advocates for the widow and the orphan, the stranger and the poor. The Decalogue begins with "I am the Lord your God, who brought you out of the land of Egypt . . . " (Exodus 20:2). Therefore, the motivation for the expected response from the Israelites was their own experience of deliverance, sustaining love, and special relationship with God.

Christians' response to justice issues must spring forth from their affirmation of who God is and how God relates to them. God, the Creator of all, is a good God. It was out of God's own goodness that God gave birth to creation. The whole universe is a reflection of that love. The first chapter of Genesis indicates that God felt creation to be very good. God's motive in creation is to give life. Out of God's own freedom, God chose to need the life that has been created. Thus, God creates out of grace, not out of some inadequacy; the emphasis on relationship is fundamental.

Being created in the image of God means persons are response-able to God and capable of having an I-Thou relationship with God and with one another. Secondly, persons are responsible to God because God has given human dominion over creation. Under God, we are gardeners of God's creation. In both the Old and New Testaments, persons are responsible and response-able to God. Human beings created in the image of God have the potential to conform to the image of the Son of God, Jesus Christ. Though we as Christians cannot duplicate God's personality, we may seek to be the best we can be by using Jesus of Nazareth as a role model. Personality is each person's gift from God and to God.

Humans each have an individual self. I am a somebody; God knows me by name. I am not a finished product. I am in the process of becoming who God created me to be. Because we humans have been given the gift of freedom, we are able to see that things might be other than they are. As social beings made in the image of God, humans can create and be recreated. As imaginative creatures who have a memory, understanding and will, humanity can dream and knit the past, present and future; persons thus have potential for both good and evil. Human beings live in two worlds, our Father's world and a fallen world corrupted by sin and evil due to God's having chosen to give humans the power to make choices. We are free, therefore, to choose to do right instead of wrong. We resemble God because we are free to choose what pleases us. This has been referred to as "crossroads freedom" (Weatherhead, 1972). This free will creates circumstances of evil, however, that allow God's children to be treated as nonpersons by others and by institutions.

Liberation theology reminds us that people are not poor because they are lazy or shiftless, but because society has been so structured that the poor are destined to be poor unless social transformation occurs. Many who live in poverty are not free to choose their own destiny in this life. "Checkbook freedom," sadly enough, is freedom of circumstances which permits relatively few of the human race to enjoy the fruits of the earth, while the majority remains enslaved by poverty (Micks, 1982).

The problem of how our faith in God's love and power fit with our experience in a world of evil and suffering confronts every believer sooner or later. The problems may become so acute that it threatens faith that God does guide and govern the world. Such biblical passages as Romans 8:28, "We know that in everything God works for good . . . ," (see also Psalm 23) assures the Christian that God is active in the world and imminent through the Holy Spirit. God does not just observe but cares for and works through creation.

Affirming God's providence means one rejects fatalism and sheer chance and believes in freedom. God's will is carried out in the structure and process of the creation in which we live. Structure implies limits. The will of God in specific circumstances must be seen in the context of God's larger will or purpose. Beyond these structures, free and finite humans are dependent upon God. Leslie Weatherhead defines three types of will of God. First, things happen that God does not intend but allows. Second, the circumstantial will of God occurs because of the way things have developed up to a point; it may be that there are no other options. Jesus sought in the garden to determine God's will under circumstances that existed at that time and discovered the ultimate will of God for him was at hand. Weatherhead says God's ultimate will is the vision of the coming Kingdom of God in which what God intends and how creatures respond to God are no longer at odds (1972).

When we pray, we are asking God to show us options. When someone has reached the limits of possiblity, we, as God's representatives, must be there to remind that person of God's gracious sustenance. God's Son, God in earthly form, chose to live out His human existence with the oppressed. In His life, Jesus exhibits a powerfulness that contradicts all one's assumptions about power. Power does not dominate; it serves. To some, it appears to be weakness. Jesus did not preserve Himself or impose His will upon others. In His teachings and in His life, Jesus stands

42

completely opposed to all power that victimizes, to all the energies of violence against innocent people. Jesus' mission was to the poor, to the weak and to the dying; the poor were fed, the sinful forgiven, the weak strengthened, and the dying made alive (McGill, 1968). In taking the side of those who suffer, God did not abolish the hurts of human existence but rather willed to be a God who suffers with creation and who even participates in human suffering. Jurgen Moltmann acclaims that an appropriate Christian theology sees the cross of an outcast and forsaken Christ as the visible revelation of God's being for humanity in the reality of his world. Thus, true theology and true knowledge of God lies in Christ, the crucified one (Moltmann, 1974).

The story of the Exodus provides evidence that salvation is tangible and visible as well as spiritual. For the Hebrews, redemption meant prosperity and victory over oppression as well as salvation from sin and guilt. Ironically, most theologians have chosen to emphasize the other-worldly dimension of redemption, thus making liberation theology necessary (Moyd, 1979).

The cries of victims are the voice of God. God's identification with victims, even His own Son, was not a passive acceptance of suffering but an empowering transformation whereby the forces of death and evil were overcome through the resurrection (Lamb, 1982). It is through faith in the resurrection of Jesus Christ that hope begins, the expectation of something that has not yet happened.

We are summoned as disciples of faith, hope and love to live out God's identification with victims. We will be judged by the extent to which we respond to the voices of these cries (Lamb, 1982). Concrete human suffering destroys all innocence, all neutrality, every attempt to say, "It wasn't I; there is nothing I could do; I didn't know." In the face of suffering, one is either with the victim or the executioner . . . there is no other option (Soelle, 1984). "For I was hungry and you gave me no food. I was thirsty and you gave me no drink. I was a stranger and you did not welcome me, naked and you did not clothe me, sick and in prison and you did not visit me" (Matt. 22:42f).

The world is a marketplace of human need. The above theological discussion comes out of a struggle to find an explanation for why people have to suffer and to define the role of the church in that suffering. Life is not fair. Anguish and heartbreak have not been evenly distributed. No one has arrived at a theodicy that satisfactorily responds to these haunting questions. Hope comes out of honestly confronting these difficult questions, however. Perhaps the sense of outrage and indignation one feels when observing or experiencing injustice and oppression, the feeling of compassion for the suffering, is the surest proof of God's reality. Such hope will give way to despair, however, if it is not rooted in specific action. This is the pivotal juncture for successful Christian ministry. When people are without hope, the church needs to be there to encourage, intercede for, and love as Christ has loved us. The Bible certainly does not keep us in the dark as to how God's people should relate to the poor. There are over 400 verses in the scriptures that indicate God's concern for the poor (Claerbaut, 1983). David Claerbaut describes the major sin of Sodom as being its insensitivity to the poor and deprived within that decadent city (Claerbaut, 1983). The great prophet-farmer Amos from Teko had harsh words for his hearers in the Northern Kingdom, pronouncing judgment upon them because they hated the poor and turned them away from the gates of the city. They indeed had trampled upon the needy. God's message to these Israelites was, "I hate, I despise your feasts and your offerings are not acceptable . . . " (Amos 5:21). Their only hope was to "seek the Lord and live." They were to "Let justice roll down like waters and righteousness like an everflowing stream" (Amos 5:24). The central theme of Amos was that the rich were getting richer and the poor were getting poorer, a theme no less applicable today. The psalmist said, "Blessed (happy) are those who are kind toward the poor" (Proverbs 29:17). "The good man knows the rights of the poor, the Godless man does not care" (Proverbs 29:7). Included in the moral laws of Moses was a protection of minorities such as slaves. Debts were to be forgiven every seven years. The fields were to be left fallow so the poor could glean the fields after harvest. Against this backdrop of Old Testament law, one can see the same trends woven into the life of the early church as they shared all things in common.

The ultimate model for local church social ministries is found in the life and ministry of Jesus Christ. In His inaugural address, Jesus defined His own mission to the marginal people of society. Luke records this visit to his hometown of Nazareth (Luke 4:18-19). As Jesus read from the scroll of the prophet Isaiah, He set forth the five goals of His mission on earth: preach good news to the poor, proclaim liberty for prisoners, recover the sight of the blind, release the oppressed and bring hope to the hopeless who need the Lord's favor (Colemen, 1984). Jesus has called His people to deliver the same message. This good news is that God sides with the poor of this present life. Jesus said, "I have come that you might have life and have it more abundantly."

This message must both be preached and lived out through caring ministries that meet human needs. Unmistakably, the New Testament teaches that those who are in a right relationship with God will respond to the cries of hurting people. Compassion requires redemptive suffering as modeled for us in the Son of Man, Jesus Christ.

Oostlyk (1983) lists eleven reasons for Christians to help the poor and the disadvantaged, beginning with (1) obedience to God (1 John 5:3) and (2) following Christ's example. (3) Christ meets us in the needs of the poor. "Anyone who takes care of a little child like this is caring for me" (Luke 9:46-48). (4) Helping others creates opportunities for spiritual growth. (5) Identification with Christ means participating in human suffering (2 Cor. 1:3-5). (6) Following Christ means taking on the role of servant and emulating his example of servanthood. (7) Such a lifestyle brings blessings and rewards (Proverbs 19:17) and (8) escape from God's judgment (Lam. 3:34-36). (9) Responding to human needs creates living proof of a vital faith. "Faith that does not result in good deeds is not real faith" (James 2:30). Of course, the ultimate reason for helping those in need is (10) to abolish anything that does not bring glory to God, such as prejudice, oppression, or inequality (1 Cor. 10:31). Finally (11) responding to the needs of the poor and disadvantaged lends evidence of our love for God (1 John 3:17-18). Love in action, with no strings attached, is the supreme act of love for God.

The account of Jesus' post-resurrection visit to his disciples by the Sea of Galilee presents what is perhaps the best biblical case study for doing Christian social ministries in a local church. On this occasion, Jesus asked his impulsive but loving disciple Simon Peter a very personal, probing question, "Do you love me?" Peter's response was "Yes, Lord." To this response, Jesus said, "Feed my sheep" (John 21:15). Twice more, Jesus reiterated that if Simon Peter loved Him, he would feed His sheep. Who are the sheep? Jesus was very specific about who the sheep are and which sheep need to be fed. In Matthew's gospel (25:35-45), Jesus tells us there are hungry sheep, naked sheep, sheep that are sick, sheep that are strangers and prison-bound sheep. Every single one is special to God (Baker, 1985). At the last judgment, we will be evaluated according to our response, whether we "did it unto one of the least of these" or whether we did not (Stagg, 1991). Therefore, the question is not should we minister to these sheep, but how will we do it?

How One Church Does It

I arrived at First Baptist Montgomery on July 1, 1988. My pastor's instructions were, "You are the expert. I do not know what we need; you tell us. We want a good program, so dream big. Do not be afraid to take risks." Suddenly I realized I was in a social worker's paradise. "Director of Community Ministries" became my title. The position was so new there was no job description; I wrote my own. The Director of Community Ministries assesses the needs of the community, educates the church about those needs, coordinates existing programs, develops new programs, enlists and trains volunteers to do the ministering, and provides an ongoing process of evaluation for the Community Ministries program at First Baptist.

Step 1: Getting Started - Know Your Church and Community
The first six months at First Baptist were spent assessing community needs. I visited 27 helping agencies, hospitals, and other churches in the community. I interviewed key informants, gathered census data, visited university campuses in the city, and met with government leaders and their staffs. My questions were, "What type of service does your agency/organization provide and who qualifies for your services?"; "What can First Baptist Church do to help your agency or program?"; and "What needs in this community are most pressing?" I also carefully studied the United Way's needs assessment data and any other description, including local news of the community. I was looking for gaps in services and new avenues of services for the people of First Baptist Church. Assessing the needs of the community continues; effective ministry responds to knowledge of current needs.

I also took an inventory of the church's resources. I attended meetings of mission organizations and other church groups to assess the church's individual and corporate gifts and skills. I interviewed key church leaders. I also used (and continue to use) a spiritual gifts inventory with church members who volunteer to work in the church's Christian social ministries programs. I identified potential volunteers when speaking to groups such as Sunday School classes. Developing friendships within the staff and congregation provided additional perspectives on congregational life.

I studied the church's history in its written documents and in conversations with long time church members. Such study identified aspects of the church's personality, themes, and traditions. Although First Baptist has had a long tradition of being a very caring and giving church, the church has not coordinated these ministries. Even though the assessment was not complete, I began to help concerned church members find their niche in social ministries.

In addition to my learning about the church, this assessment phase enabled the church to learn about me. The pastor had prepared the church for my coming. A reception in my honor welcomed me into the church. I continue to speak in a worship service once a month, making me visible to the congregation, giving credibility to Christian social ministries, and providing a means for presenting the community's needs to the church.

Step 2: Data Analysis and Problem Identification
The following conclusions were drawn from the community needs assessment:

1. Montgomery County has one of the highest infant mortality rates in the state of Alabama.
2. There is insufficient decent and affordable low-income housing.
3. Substance abuse, teenage pregnancy, and spouse and child abuse are critical problems.
4. The community has inadequate public transportation to and from social service agencies.
5. One out of three adults in Montgomery County is functionally illiterate.
6. There are 10 correctional institutions within a twenty-five mile radius of Montgomery.

All of these problems relate to poverty. Hence, the church decided to focus its ministry on what and how First Baptist Church can address the issues of poverty and its effects on the church's neighbors. From this point forward, there has been an underlying assumption that we wanted to design programs that would make a real difference in people's lives; a bandaid approach to ministry is not acceptable.

Analyzing data and problem identification can be time-consuming and brings to the surface far more problems than any church congregation can or should address. Prioritizing community problems can be painful since one will often be choosing between equally urgent needs (Miller & Wilson, 1985). Overcoming this dilemma can be accomplished by joining with other helping professionals. For example, Montgomery County's high infant mortality rate can best be addressed by the medical profession and is currently being done through a multidisciplinary approach called the Gift of Life Program. First Baptist and other churches are taking a supportive role by supplying volunteers to do home visits, making baby layettes, and participating in the Adopt-a-Grandchild and First Step Programs.

Information about community needs was and continues to be shared through seminars, workshops, guest speakers, a newsletter, and presentations to various groups within the church.

47

Step 3: Feasibility Study - How can the Church Respond?

The feasibility of the church's response to a community problem must be studied carefully. Does the problem lie within the realm of the church's mission statement? What will be the costs? Will the membership respond by committing their time and financial resources? Building a program run by church members means offering a variety of volunteer activities, both short term and long term, for the variety of volunteer interests and skills. This is an impossible task without knowing the church and its volunteers. For example, First Baptist members appreciate the importance of education as one way of breaking the poverty cycle. Literacy and tutoring programs thus were readily embraced as a response to community needs. Our Literacy Missions Center is the first in the city to be located in a local church. Literacy and tutorial programs work well in congregations with large numbers of professional people who have both limited time for volunteer work but also a desire to serve through community ministries.

Step 4: State-of-the-Art Review - Don't Reinvent the Wheel

The church identified prison ministry as one of the areas of need in its community assessment. A juvenile correctional facility is located five miles from First Baptist. Housed at this facility is an evaluation center, an intensive care unit and a residential treatment center. A needs assessment shows little is being done to meet the spiritual and moral development needs of these adolescents. The directors of these programs, however, are very open to religious groups volunteering their services.

Addressing the issues pinpointed in the needs assessment began with a review of professional resources. These include the journal *Social Work and Christianity*, other professional social work literature, information gleaned at professional conferences and workshops where advances in the field are presented, and key informants (Thomas, 1984).

A review of religious literature on prison ministry revealed nothing written from a church social work perspective. Thus, we developed our own approach to the needs of these adolescents.

Troubled adolescents often suffer from a great sense of loss, isolation and severe low self-esteem. Due to exploitation, molestation, rejection or other types of abuse, their lives often become highly disorganized and dysfunctional. Theoretically, most trouble adolescents have not developed a cognitive buffer against anti-social influences and temptations. Thus, sociomoral immaturity puts such children at a much higher risk for delinquency (Gibbs, 1984).

To aid troubled adolescents at this facility who lag behind in their moral development, I enlisted and trained volunteers to lead sociomoral dilemma groups. The dilemma groups model engages the troubled adolescent in thinking, reasoning and reflecting upon difficult real life dilemmas. A major emphasis is placed on consequences of choices made and the effect of such choices on others (Ferguson, 1988).

Step 5: Program Design - Caring Love in Action

Our community ministries program at First Baptist has unfolded by matching a need in the community with a program designed to meet that need, as with the clients of the juvenile detention facility and other correctional facilities. We also work hard at having a spirit of cooperation with agencies and groups in the community by complementing what they are doing.

There are ten correctional facilities within a tri-county area. This system is very open to Christian ministry. We have developed a working relationship with the chaplains of these institutions; they know they can call on First Baptist for assistance whenever necessary. Prison Fellowship, a national organization based in Washington, D.C., has helped our development of prison ministries; they provided our first in-service training sessions. Now we have trained our own leadership to do our semi-annual workshops. Volunteers in the correctional facilities lead small groups, self-help groups, Bible study groups, literacy programs, and counsel one on one. Others serve on boards and committees at the institutions.

Providing this caring connection between church and community often means filling in the gaps left by public agencies. For example, our Department of Human Resources refers clients to our Emergency Assistance program when they do not qualify for that agency's services.

My role as church social worker includes brokering, advocating, motivating, teaching and training, and designing courses of action. The ministries themselves belong to the church and volunteers, however. Functioning committees plan and advise each individual component of our Community Ministries Program. This method involves more people in the planning and carrying out of each aspect of our program. Job descriptions and goals and objectives are formulated by each committee. This process allows volunteers to use their expertise while providing a variety of ministries.

The prison committee is made up of a criminal lawyer, a special education specialist, and three other lay volunteers. One committee member serves on the advisory board of a juvenile institution and another is an area representative for Prison Fellowship.

Our AIDS Task Force consists of one mother whose son died of AIDS, a volunteer from an AIDS support group, an attorney who has represented people with AIDS, and others who are simply concerned about what the church can do minister with AIDS victims. This group planned an area-wide conference on AIDS attended by 130 clergypersons in our area. They invited Bill Amos, author of *When AIDS Comes to the Church* (1988) to speak to the congregation in a worship service. The task force also helped establish an AIDS Task Force in a neighboring church.

Our first Community Ministries pilot project began shortly after my arrival. The first project needed to be a very positive and successful venture in order to encourage further response and commitment of church members to social ministries. First Baptist Church's first Literacy Mission Center was born. After researching literacy programs, I engaged a consultant to train our volunteers using a method for teaching adult non-readers (Laubach, 1981). Next, we set a target date for beginning the ministry. A strategy for recruitment of students included public service announcements on local radio stations. I contacted the Department of Human Resources, public health services, adult education offices, and other helping agencies. Local community centers and emergency assistance programs also made referrals. A job description was developed for the volunteer Director of the Literacy Missions Center. This person's responsibilities include planning and organizing training workshops, recruiting students and volunteer teachers, matching students and teachers, keeping records, providing materials, and promoting the program.

A biblical basis for becoming involved in the eradication of illiteracy and the plan of action were communicated to the church through our Woman's Missionary Union and through myself and my pastor from the pulpit. The response was tremendous; First Baptist now has 76 trained volunteer teachers.

In addition to our Literacy Mission Center, two and one-half years after First Baptist Church hired its first social worker, the Community Ministries Program consists of the following areas of ministry:

1. **Emergency Assistance Program** - Clients are seen by the social worker two days a week. Volunteers help screen and interview applicants. Referrals come from every helping agency in town, including churches. The funding for this program, maintained separately from the Community Ministries operating budget,

comes from designated gifts or a monthly offering for this purpose. Last year's offerings exceeded $100,000.

2. **International Conversational English School** - Every Thursday approximately 75 persons who want to learn English come to First Baptist Church for Conversational English classes. Coordinating this program involves working with the Montgomery Baptist Association of Churches, Maxwell Air Force base, and local residents. In addition to providing the meeting place, the church trains volunteer teachers and childcare workers; they plan refreshments and special holiday activities. Last year, First Baptist served as host for the International Family Orientation program for Maxwell Air University; First Baptist Church hosted world leaders from 36 different countries.

3. **Prison Ministry** - We have two small group meetings weekly at the state's Juvenile Evaluation Center located in our city. In addition, we provide three Sunday worship services, two in the chapel and one in the intensive care unit. Volunteers also provide three Bible studies weekly at the Federal prison in our community. Individual counseling is provided by other volunteers at the women's prison nearby. A literacy program was started and is being maintained in another institution. One First Baptist volunteer has given so much time to the chaplains' program that the new chapel was named after him.

First Baptist participates in work release community projects with Prison Fellowship. We also work with the county court system providing community service projects for parolees and first offenders. The church will also coordinate prison visits when the Billy Graham Crusade comes to Montgomery. Annually, the church provides Christmas gifts for over 100 children of inmates.

The church also participated in the development of "Montgomery Neighbors Who Care," a shared ministry of local Montgomery churches. The program provides physical, emotional, and spiritual support to victims of property crime.

4. **Tutoring Program** - On Wednesday evening, children at risk of school failure come to the church from a neighboring low-income housing community for the evening meal and one-on-one tutoring.

5. **S.T.E.P. (Strategies to Elevate People)** - This is a joint effort involving 15 Montgomery churches. First Baptist has had a major role in establishing this ecumenical program to mobilize Montgomery's churches to work with the poor of our city. A

51

white church is paired with a Black church to work together in each low-income housing community in the city. Clergy and lay volunteers work with community leaders, agencies, schools and community residents to make the housing communities better places to live. Each team of churches is encouraged to be innovative in their approach.

First Baptist developed a Mom's Program, a self-help group for single parents, parenting classes, drug education, friendship teams, tutoring program and other activities for the residents in a 600 unit public housing facility near our church. S.T.E.P. provides six scholarships to state colleges for graduating seniors from these low income housing communities.

6. **Peanut Butter Ministry** - First Baptist has many transient persons, but we noticed many did not eat the food we provided. Therefore, we began providing peanut butter sandwiches. Peanut butter is healthy, convenient to store, and liked by many. Through the grapevine, transient persons soon learn that peanut butter sandwiches are available at First Baptist. A group of senior citizens keep the ministry supplied with plenty of sandwiches. This is their way of "feeding the hungry."

7. **Partnership with Habitat for Humanity** - First Baptist became the first church in Montgomery to finance and build a complete house in partnership with Habitat for Humanity. Volunteers from First Baptist Church also help with labor, tools, and financial support on other Habitat projects.

8. **Bible Clubs** - We have weekly Bible clubs in four Boy's and Girl's Clubs in Montgomery. These clubs provide a sense of belonging to a group while including Bible study and refreshments. Volunteers for these clubs come from First Baptist's youth group.

Other special events include holiday parties and projects such as Christmas parties for the AIDS Unit at one of the prisons, for Headstart children, and for mentally ill patients in a halfway house. When a church group wants to be involved in social ministry, I assess their interests and locate a place of service. I encourage them to adopt a family and continue in ministry with them until they can make a difference. One shot projects, such as giving food baskets at Christmas, are discouraged.

The church sees me as a resource person who is aware of the needs of the community. At the present time, I serve on the Board of Directors at the Family Guidance Center of Montgomery, Neighbors Who Care, the Advisory Board of the State Juvenile Facility, the Advisory

Board for Habitat for Humanity, the Council of S.T.E.P., and the Community Council for the United Way. These opportunities for service present me with direct access to valuable information that can be used to develop new ministries at First Baptist through our Community Ministries Program.

Observations and Conclusions

From these initial experiences at First Baptist Church, Montgomery, the following generalizations can be drawn which may be useful to social workers on the staff of other congregations.

I. **Both the church and community must be seen as a client system. Immediately upon arrival, one needs to establish credibility within both the church and the community.** As a result of my developing a positive professional relationship with the helping network of the community, these agencies see First Baptist Church as an ally. Therefore, referrals come from all over the city on a daily basis.

II. **Along with the commitment to serve the congregation should be a commitment to serve the community.** Belonging to groups outside the church gives one the opportunity to share expertise with others in the community.

My first week at First Baptist Church, a church member invited me to attend a meeting of "One Montgomery." This interracial group meets once a week for breakfast at a local hospital. The group works to improve life for all Montgomerians with particular emphasis on the elimination of friction based on race. Belonging to this group has probably helped me to know Montgomery better than anything I have done since my arrival. I have met and become friends with community leaders, including such people as the owner of the local newspaper, a former ambassador, clergypersons, and business leaders. In turn, I have served as program chairperson and served on the planning committee for a community conference entitled *One Montgomery-Building Bridges.*

III. **Assessing needs, planning and evaluation are basic principles in effective ministry.** A common mistake is to be so interested in ministry that one sees preparation a waste of time. After all, Jesus took thirty years to prepare for a three year ministry. Why should we take our work less seriously? Planning allows one to be more efficient with resources God has made available to us.

53

Similarly, evaluation should be integral to church social work practice. At a pivotal point in his ministry, Jesus took his disciples aside and did a survey. "Whom do you say that I am?" (Luke 9:20). Jesus wanted to know if he was accomplishing his goals. On another occasion, Jesus said, "By their fruits you shall know them" (Matthew 7:16). He was referring to tangible things that could be observed and measured.

After every special event, volunteers and I evaluate what went well, what we could have done better, and what will be changed before we do this again. Sometimes evaluation includes the pastor as in the case of a conference we did, "Ministering to Families with Special Needs." Attendance was not good; our evaluation helped us to pinpoint the reasons. First, we had set the date on the day of a major football game in our area. Second, it was determined that we had rushed our people into something for which they were not prepared. We resolved to spend more time preparing the congregation before another similar conference and find better ways of promoting and communicating who should attend the next conference.

IV. **Match your strengths and those of your church with the most pressing needs in your community.** Ministries based on church's strengths will most effectively communicate the Gospel's Good News, whether through food, clothing, friendship, childcare, or other support programs.

V. **Affirm, strengthen, and maintain the connection between the services being offered and the faith which provides the impetus for service.** The caring connection between First Baptist Church, Montgomery, and its community can perhaps best be illustrated by telling Missy's story.

Missy is 27 years old. She is the white mother of two bi-racial children, ages 2 and 4. Missy was adopted at age two. Between the ages of six and fifteen she was sexually abused by her adopted father. Missy ran away from home at fifteen, never to return. At age sixteen, she began a relationship with a young man who had a history of mental illness and drug abuse. For the next six years, there were good times and bad times. There were brushes with the law, ranging from speeding tickets to accessory to armed robbery. Her live-in boyfriend served time in prison. Then there was a legal marriage and children.

I met Missy when she came to the church for emergency assistance. She and her husband were expecting their second child any day. Neither had a job; their only income was the husband's supplemental security income check. There was no furniture in the house, no food, little clothing, and the utilities were about to be cut off. The church paid the utilities and gave her clothing, food, and furniture.

I next saw Missy a year later. Her situation had changed very little, except now she was trying to work as a waitress and care for her mentally ill husband and two small children. She had no transportation to or from her job. There was no busline near her home and no money for a babysitter. She had no choice but to leave her children with their father or his family, neither capable of providing appropriate care. By this point Missy wanted to do whatever it took to take responsibility and control of her own life. An assessment of Missy's needs led to her spending many hours with volunteers from a Sunday School class that "adopted" Missy and her family. The class provided work, transportation, childcare, financial planning, and legal advice.

During this period, her husband broke his parole through drug use and robbery. The church provided legal aid to Missy that resulted in his reincarceration. Yet another tragedy occurred. Missy was raped at gunpoint in the presence of her children by the boyfriend of her mother-in-law. She was taken to the spouse abuse shelter for counseling.

As the caring relationship continued to develop between Missy and the church, other problems were revealed. Missy, out of desperation, had written bad checks and had several outstanding arrest warrants in another state. The First Baptist Community Ministries program paid these debts.

At the time of this writing, Missy has been cleared of all charges against her. She has a new job and a car donated by a church member. Missy has just enrolled in her first semester of college. Missy's story illustrates how one church's caring connection changes lives and offers new beginnings to "one of the least of these."

REFERENCES

Amos, William (1988). *When AIDS comes to the church*. Philadelphia, Pennsylvania: Westminster Press.

Baker, Benjamin (1985). *Feeding the sheep*. Nashville, Tennessee: Broadman Press.

Blackburn, Deana (1983). *Love in action*. Birmingham, Alabama: Woman's Missionary Union.

Claerbaut, David (1983). *Urban ministry*. Grand Rapids, Michigan: Zondervan Publishing House.

Coleman, Lymon (1987). *Serendipity New Testament*. Grand Rapids, Michigan: Zondervan Press.

Ferguson, Jane (1988). Sociomoral dilemma group model. In Patricia L. Bailey (Ed.), *Models for ministry*. Atlanta, Georgia: Carver School of Church Social Work - Paul R. Adkins Institute for Research & Training in Church Social Work and Home Mission Board of the Southern Baptist Convention.

Gibbs, John, Arnold, Keven, and Ahlborn, Helen (1984). Facilitation of sociomoral reasoning in delinquents. *Journal of Consulting and Clinical Psychology*, 52, (1), 37-45.

Haugk, Kenneth (1984). *Christian caregiving, a way of life*. Minneapolis, Minnesota: Augsburg Publishing House.

Keith-Lucas, Alan (1956). *Your neighbor as yourself*. Atlanta, Georgia: Presbyterian Church of the U.S.A.

Lamb, Matthew (1982). *Solidarity with victims*. New York: Crossroad Publishing.

Larsen, John (1981). Applying Kohlberg's theory of moral development in group care settings. *Child Welfare*. 60 (10), 659-667.

Laubach, Frank (1981). *Laubach way to reading*. Syracuse, New York: New Readers Press.

McGill, Arthur (1968). *Suffering: a test of theological method*. Pennsylvania: Fortress Press.

May, Herbert and Metzger, Bruce (Eds.) (1965). *The Oxford Annotated Bible with the Apocrypha*. New York: Oxford Press.

Micks, Marianna (1982). *Our search for identity*. Pennsylvania: Fortress Press.

Millery, Kenneth and Wilson, Mary (1985). *The church that cares*. Valley Forge, Pennsylvania: Judson Press.

Mitchell, Marcia (1988). *Giftedness: Discovering your areas of strength*. Minneapolis, Minnesota: Bethany House Publishers.

Moltmann, Jurgen (1974). *The crucified God: the cross of Christ as the foundation and criticism of Christian theology*. New York: Harper and Row.

Moltmann, Jurgen (1967). *Theology of hope*. London: SCM Press.

Moyd, Olin (1979). *Redemption in black theology*. Valley Forge, Pennsylvania: Judson Press.

Munson, Robert, and Blincoe, M.M. (1984). Evaluation of a residential treatment center for emotionally disturbed adolescents, *Adolescence*. 19, 254.

Neuber, K. (1980). *Needs assessment: A model for community planning*. Beverly Hills, California: Sage Publications..

Nelson-Pallmeyer, Jack (1986). *The politics of compassion*. Mary Knoll, New York: Orbis Books.

Oostlyk, Harvy (1983). *Step one, the Gospel and the ghetto*. Basking Ridge, New Jersey: Sonlife International Inc.

Soelle, Dorothee (1984). *To work and to love: A theology of creation*. Pennsylvania: Fortress Press.

Spotts, Dwight, and Veerman, David (1987). *Reaching troubled youth*. USA: Victor Books.

Staff, Frank (1991). Personal communication.

Thomas, Edwin (1984). *Designing interventions for helping professions*. Beverly Hills, California: Sage Publications.

Tupper, Frank (1985). *God*. Unpublished manuscript. Louisville, Kentucky: Southern Baptist Theological Seminary.

Weatherhead, Leslie (1972). *The will of God*. Tennessee: Abingdon Press.

Wilson, Marlene (1983). *How to mobilize church volunteers*. Minneapolis, Minnesota: Augsburg Publishing Company.

Wilson, Marlene (1990). *You can make a difference!* Boulder, Colorado: Volunteer Management Associates.

CHAPTER 4

Social Work Practice in Community Ministries

by Patricia L. Bailey*

Emergence of a Movement

The Ecumenical Community Ministries Movement resulted from the merger of several forces in the 1970s. First, the ecumenical movement in general was at its height. Members in mainline Protestant churches and Jewish synagogues were being encouraged to move to ecumenical structures. Vatican II had already energized the Roman Catholic parishes for social justice.

Second, the federal government was cutting monies for social services, asking local communities to pick up more and more of the costs of human services. These budget cuts have continued and increased through eight years of the Reagan administrations to the present. Peter L. Berger and Richard John Neuhaus (1977) wrote of four mediating structures–neighborhood, family, church, and voluntary associations–institutions standing between the individual's private life and the large institutions of public life. The national rhetoric was clear; these mediating structures would need to pick up the human service slack caused by the federal budget cuts.

A third social force generating the need for ecumenical community ministries was the inability of individual congregations to meet the growing needs of their communities. In order to muster a sufficient volunteer and resource base, churches who wanted to respond significantly to community needs had to include other churches in their efforts, whether in their denomination or ecumenically. For example, one food ministry program depended upon a pool of more than 150 volunteers, of which only about 40 came from the sponsoring United Methodist church. The remainder of the volunteers represented members of other United Methodist churches, other Protestant and Catholic churches, Jews, and persons wanting to serve because of their personal values who were not identified with any congregation (Rendle & Sanders, 1987). Certainly, the time had long passed when individual congregations could meet all

---

* Patricia L. Bailey, ACSW, is Associate Professor of Social Work, Carver School of Church Social Work, The Southern Baptist Theological Seminary, Louisville, Kentucky.

the needs of a community (Dalton, 1979; Bailey, 1988; and Bennett, 1967). Community needs had become more complex with urbanization, and a comprehensive strategy of ecumenical cooperation for planning ministry was needed (Dalton, 1979).

> Individual churches do not have the staff nor the facilities to do the essential research or to analyze the assembled social facts . . . . If protestantism is to serve the community adequately in terms of the vast new population, the unprecedented mobility . . . the exhaustion of funds due to excessive demands plus inflated building costs, and the nationwide experience of neighborhood deterioration, it must cooperate (North, 1953).

Even congregations that would not otherwise be oriented to ecumenism valued cooperating to organize emergency assistance and child care in their communities. Congregations from all points on the theological and political spectrum–from conservative to liberal–responded to the biblical mandate–feed the hungry, lift up the fallen, visit the sick and imprisoned, and clothe the naked.

Historically, churches and synagogues had provided social ministry in neighborhoods and communities, but they had not formed inter-faith structures for service delivery. For example, during the immigration periods, Roman Catholic parishes developed styles reflecting the dominant neighborhood group–Irish, Polish, Italian, Mexican. Lutheran and Protestant churches also had a nationality orientation. Synagogues gave Jews their own institution in a world that was often hostile, and Jewish community centers related to residents concentrated in particular neighborhoods. In the American Black community, churches have always been the center of community life, whether they were large denominational churches, such as Baptists, or storefront congregations (Hallman, 1984).

It was not by chance that the church involved itself in the social fabric of the community. The first verse that many children learn in Christian religious education is John 3:16: "For God so loved the world . . . ." The people of God are to serve in the world. Findley Edge (1971) put it plainly:

> What really does it mean to be the People of God? They are a people who believe, certainly. They are a people who are "good" in terms of personal morality, certainly. But these things do not constitute the heart of the matter. The uniqueness of God's people is that they are called to a mission.

John R.W. Stott (1975) said that the mission of the church includes everything which God sends people into the world to do, including social action.

The ecumenical movement of the 1960s and 1970s generated a new context for ministry praxis. Theologians like Karl Rahner (1974) called for institutional changes that would be ecumenically oriented. This new context for practice has been referred to in a variety of ways: ecumenical community ministries, cluster ministries, community ministries, or cooperative community ministries. These describe a group of two or more churches of more than one denomination which come together for the purpose of providing ministry within a specific community (Dalton, 1979; Bailey, 1988; Bos, 1988). A community includes "people within a limited territory possessing shared values, common interests, and norms of conduct, engaging in social interaction and mutual aid, and having their own groups, associations, and institutions to help meet their basic needs" (Hallman, 1984, p. 34).

Community Ministries

Community ministries organize themselves legally as non-profit agencies, a status which requires a board with officers and a budget for the agency. The ministry typically has central intake procedures, a director who coordinates services, and a variety of programming, including emergency assistance, child care, services for senior citizens, counseling for individuals and families, as well as community organizing interventions planned around common community concerns such as utility rates for low income families or housing needs (Bailey, 1988; Bos, 1988; Hough, 1988). "Ideally, this caring about the community extends to all its people and institutions, its economy, its ecology, and everything that impinges upon its general well-being" (Bos, 1985, p. 125).

Carasco, Reed, and Wendorf (1991) offer helpful principles of church-based community organizing that can be applied to community ministries. First, issues that affect some members of the community need to be framed as community concerns: "Our community and its pain are our business, and our pain does not belong to just one person" (p. 59). Second, community organizing and community building take committed work over extended time before results can be determined: You plant a garden and the first thing you want to do is harvest; but it takes a lot of care, nurturing, and work before you see the results. Evidence of results from work invested is often slow and sparse in the early months (Hough, 1988).

Funding for community ministries comes from donations from neighborhood congregations and public and private sources. The agency usually charges fees for services such as child care, senior adult trips, and counseling. The more stable community ministries often assess rates for congregations according to size. Those ministries that depend instead on voluntary contributions from churches find planning their budgets particularly difficult. Contracts for services from state agencies through federal block grants provide funding for the ministries as well as grants from community, foundation, and corporation sources. Community businesses also can serve as funding sources. As is always the case, the more diversified the funding sources, the more stable the agency. Organizations that are dependent on one or two sources for funding are more likely to experience financial crisis.

Community ministry staffs include professional social workers and volunteers from the congregations and neighborhood at large. The smaller, newer ministries often can afford only a part-time director and rely heavily on volunteers. The larger, older ministries may have as many as sixty staff members (Hough, 1988). Use of both volunteers and professional staff have supportive rationale. From a biblical perspective, God calls believers to serve and advocate for justice. The community ministry provides an ideal context for the fulfillment of this mandate by volunteering congregational members. On the other hand, a professional social work practice perspective values the staffing of the agency with paid professionals and limited numbers of volunteers, in order to ensure the quality of services.

Issues in Community Ministries

The community ministry model is valid only as long as it provides an effective means of doing Christ's work in the world (Dalton, 1974). "History is replete with stories of disaster for organizations which have lost touch with their constituent units" (Hough, 1988, p. 51). There is a danger of community ministries losing their church identity as they grow and mature from small organizations staffed primarily by volunteers. When the organization expands its programs with professional staff, the link with congregations is often weakened and the agency becomes more like other community based professional social work agencies. The organization loses its identity and function as a tool for ministry. The community ministry is strongest when lay leadership generates interventions to meet neighborhood and community needs. Ministry programs serve as the means for bringing persons together in personal relationships to form

61

community for the sake of the Kingdom of God. Activities which involve volunteers often result in good neighboring. Neighboring involves exchanges of services and information among those living near one another. Even a heterogeneous neighborhood can achieve a sense of community through institutional connections and joint action on common problems (Hallman, 1984).

In order to develop this sense of community as well as to respond to community needs, most community ministries as well as other social work organizations enlist the services of volunteers. Unfortunately, volunteers sometimes feel that they are somehow better than the clients they serve; clients are not empowered by help from volunteers with this attitude. Volunteer positions thus need to be structured so that volunteers learn experientially that all are equal in God's sight, and that volunteers have much to learn from one another and from clients, regardless of their station in life. The Judeo-Christian norm is a leveling one.

Community ministries need processes for discovering gifts both of congregation members and clients and then need to generate interventions to allow the practice of gifts. An example illustrates: an assessment of the neighborhood reveals that many older women are isolated. A volunteer, perhaps one of these women, is encouraged and helped to offer a quilting group in the neighborhood. Outreach brings some of the women together the same day each week. The outcome is socialization, making a quilt together which can be sold; friendships emerge. This approach utilizes group social work approaches and methods.

Community ministries also need basic volunteer services such as emergency assistance workers and child care providers, but all too often, these volunteers are not personally involved at any level with their neighbors. Persons are empowered, however, when they discover that their issues are shared by others. Together, "clients" and "volunteers" who are enabled to develop personal relationship with one another exchange life experiences, demythologize systems, and empower themselves. In this approach to community ministry, the role of the staff is to organize, plan, evaluate, and provide crisis intervention if needed. The staff person need not be available each time the group meets. The quilters, for example, can meet short term or long term according to their wishes. Volunteers need not do the same ministry all the time. "Church members see themselves on both the giving and the receiving ends of their services" (Bos, 1985, p. 125).

As an example of a developed community ministries system, Louisville, Kentucky, now has fourteen community ministries which use the postal zip codes to establish their boundaries with one another and ensure service to the entire metropolitan area. This also allows the county to provide funds for emergency assistance to the agencies with uniformity in each community. There is also an Association of Community Ministries which serves as forum for the discussion of common concerns. In the last few years, for example, all of the Louisville community ministries have joined forces on advocacy projects concerning utility rates for low-income families. A Fund for Community Ministries for joint fund-raising keeps inter-ministry competition to a minimum (Bos, 1988; Hough, 1988). Louisville hosted the first national consultation on community ministries in October 1983 (Bos, 1985).

As community ministries multiply throughout the nation in urban and rural settings, an ecology of ministries can generate new learning and experience for the church. A community ministry in Hazard, Kentucky, serves Appalachian people; it would have something to contribute to and learn from a community ministry in Cincinnati, a city to which Appalachian peoples have immigrated for generations. The unchanging claim remains: There is one God and one church; the unity of the church is a worthy goal (Bos, 1988). "It is for the sake of the whole world that the church must be not simply united but form a visible unity, based on ecclesial structures which portray and express what the Gospel is about, namely the Kingdom of God" (Ziziolas, 1988, p. 42).

Limitations and Opportunities

There are limitations to what community ministry can do. Because of budgetary needs, it is tempting to seek every possible grant, regardless of community needs or agency mission. As one grant after another is gained, professional staff is hired; the link between the community ministry and the congregations/synagogues may be stretched until it is in name and assessed contribution only. Bos (1985) points out that community ministries pay a price for acceptance, survival, and effective working bonds with churches and synagogues. Often, that price includes a narrowing of vision concerning social mission and ecumenical/interfaith relations. Hough (1988) has also pointed out that political activity will put community ministries in a vulnerable position. Involvement in political issues needs to be considered carefully so as not to risk the wide enterprise of community ministry.

On the other hand, community ministries offer a genuine chance for ecumenical action. Bos hopes that "churches in a given area will aspire to an image of cooperation, service, and advocacy on behalf of a local community where justice and peace are hallmarks" (Bos, 1988, p 594). It can be the best of community based services. Bonded by theological intention, community ministries can provide services and care to and with neighbors and friends.

Community ministries can provide a unified voice for the people of the community as they give mutual support, share resources, and develop a centralized strategy (Dalton, 1988). "Religious institutions are in a unique position to affect the lives of a large proportion of Americans. The large number of congregation members . . . represent a significant pool of helpers . . . within large and small communities" (Pargament, 1982, p. 163). Unlike many non-sectarian community based social work practice contexts, community ministries have the chance of providing spiritual support along with physical, emotional, and social support.

Research must be done on the community ministry context to allow further professional discussion and analysis. Many of the community ministries have not formalized their processes enough to have clearly stated procedures and program evaluation data. As more programs are added and budgets increase, they will need to gather and manage data. Empirical research generated from surveys will yield specific data about size, staff issues, programming, boards, salaries, membership, and community demographics. At that point, inferential data can help develop community predictions that will be useful for future programming. The current literature on community ministries is sparse, offering descriptions but no empirical data. The best of them are based on interviews with key informants. Qualitative research using case study methodology would enrich knowledge about this context for practice along with the empirical study that needs to be done.

Community ministries have made a strong beginning. There are advantages to this context for social work practice; it provides access for services in neighborhoods through the congregations who have the trust of residents. The community ministry affords church members a means of serving their community and growing as disciples in their services for and with others. It affords the community a coordinated strategy for addressing local problems and concerns through a decentralized structure that does not overwhelm the average citizen. The service delivery of congregations can be cost effective as resources such as buildings and equipment, vans, food, and volunteers combine to provide interventions through mutual relationships. This model provides a realistic approach for the church to do God's work in the world. There is one God and one church; community ministries allow God's people to experience these relationships through mutual helping.

REFERENCES

Bailey, P. L. (1988). Southern Baptist programs of church social work. *Review & Expositor*, 85, 2, 285-290.

Bennett, G. W. (1967). *Confronting a crisis*. Atlanta: Home Mission Board of the Southern Baptist Convention.

Berger, P. & Neuhaus, R. (1977). *To empower people: The role of mediating structures in public policy*. Washington: American Enterprise Institute.

Bos, D. (1985). Community ministries: The establishment of ecumenical local mission in North American church life. *Journal of Ecumenical Studies*, 22, 1, 121-127.

Bos, D. (1988). Community ministries: The wild card in ecumenical relations and social ministry. *Journal of Ecumenical Studies*, 25, 4, 592-598.

Carasco, J. & Reed, S. and Wendorf, M. (1991). Reflections on church-based community organizing. *Church & Society*, 51, 5, 55-61.

Dalton, R. (1979). *Metropolitan ecumenical clusters as a strategy for church involvement in local ministry*. Louisville, Kentucky (Unpublished manuscript, Th.M. Thesis): The Southern Baptist Theological Seminary.

Edge F. (1971). *The greening of the church*. Waco, Texas: Word Books.

Hallman, H. W. (1984). *Neighborhoods: Their place in urban life*. Beverly Hills, CA: Sage Publications.

Hough, J. A. (1988). *The church in service to its city: An analysis of ecumenical community ministries in Louisville, Kentucky*. Louisville, Kentucky: The University of Louisville (Unpublished manuscript).

North, S. (1953). Commonsense protestantism. *The City Church*, 4, 3, 10-12.

Pargament, K. I. (1982). The interface among religion, religious support systems, and mental health. In Biegel & Naparstek (Eds.)., *Community support systems and mental health*. New York: Springer Publishing Company.

Rahner, K. (1974). *The shape of the church to come*. New York: The Seabury Press.

Rendle, G. R. and Sanders, Frank H. (1987). "Third-class" ministry: Urban ministry in the smaller city, *Quarterly Review*, 7, 2, 24-37.

Stott, J. R. W. (1975). *Christian mission*. Downers Grove, IL: Inter-Varsity Press.

Zizioulas, J. (1988). Ecumenism and the need for vision. *Sobornost*, 10, 2, 37-43.

Chapter 5

Social Work Practice in Church-Supported Child Welfare Services

*by Diana S. Richmond Garland**

The first children's institution in the United States was an orphanage established in 1729 by Ursuline nuns in New Orleans, who saw the need to care for children orphaned by the Indian massacre at Natchez (Whittaker, 1971). In 1869, a group of Baptist church women in Louisville, Kentucky, opened a children's home to care for homeless children orphaned by the Civil War. Kentucky's Baptist child care agency traces its history to that children's home. Many private child welfare agencies have similar roots in churches. Throughout child welfare history, prior to the advent of the social work profession, churches often have been the source of care for children in need. In a survey of child welfare agencies belonging to the National Association of Homes for Children, Barber recently found that over two-thirds have sponsoring organizations, and 91% of these organizations are religious in origin (Barber, 1990).

Consequently, church-supported services provide a significant segment of residential care for children. This applies to funding as well as sponsorship. Almost two-thirds (65%) of all the agencies in Barber's (1990) study (both religiously affiliated and non-religiously affiliated) receive no government funding at all.

Are services offered to children in agencies sponsored by churches, church denominations, and parachurch organizations different from those offered by state or private, nonsectarian agencies? If there are differences, in what ways are these differences reflective of limitations inherent in a church-sponsored child welfare agency? Equally important, in what ways can the church provide services that may be more difficult, for whatever reasons, to offer through public or other private agencies? To answer these questions, the author surveyed the executive directors of 128 agencies who hold membership in the National Association of Homes

* Diana Garland, ACSW, Ph.D., is Associate Professor of Social Work of the Carver School of Church Social Work, and Director of the Gheens Center for Christian Family Ministry, at The Southern Baptist Theological Seminary, Louisville, Kentucky. She has served on the staff of and as a consultant to Springmeadows Baptist Children's Home of the Kentucky Baptist Homes for Children, Inc.

66

for Children, the major professional organization for residential child care agencies. Agencies chosen for participation in the survey had names that indicated past or current religious affiliation. Of these 128 surveys, 79 responded, a return rate of 62%.

Results of the Survey: The Church as Context and Sponsor for Child Welfare Services

The Sample

Responses came from thirty states, with no state returning more than seven surveys, indicating that the sample is highly geographically representative, including agencies in states as dispersed as Alaska, Florida, Connecticut, and Oregon. Respondents represented twelve denominational groups. Baptist agencies were the most well represented in the response group, with twelve respondents indicating that they were Southern Baptist and five that they were Baptist, without further denominational designation. Two explanations can be offered for Baptists providing this relatively large percentage of the total response group (21.1%). First, the study was conducted by a clearly identified Baptist academic institution, indirectly an encouragement for Baptist agencies to respond. The numbers from each denomination are roughly comparable to the results of Barber's study, however, in which Baptists and Methodists were the most numerous (Barber, 1990).

Second, Baptists form the largest denominational group in the U.S. and, thus, may support the largest proportion of child welfare agencies. Thirteen respondents identified their agencies as Methodist and seven as Presbyterian. Other denominational affiliations included Lutheran (n = 3), United Church of Christ (n = 2), Roman Catholic, Pentecostal Holiness, Church of Christ, United Church of Christ, Christian Church, Disciples of Christ, Episcopal, and Reformed Church in America.

Over half (54%, n = 43) of the respondents identified their work settings as being sponsored partly by churches and/or religious organizations. Another 37% (n = 29) identified their work settings as *entirely* sponsored by churches and/or religious organizations. Only 8% (n = 6) identified their work setting as unrelated to any religious organization, indicating that 92% of the respondents were indeed located in settings identified to a greater or lesser extent with a church context or sponsorship. Since surveys were sent only to agencies whose names appeared to connect them to sectarian sponsorship, this is not at all surprising. Of those working in religious settings, 75% (n = 59) indicated that they were working in settings formally related to one or more church denomina-

67

tions, and 10% (n = 8) to one specific congregation. Two agencies indicated that they were related to a parachurch organization, and (5%) indicated that they were related to ecumenical organizations.

The respondents indicated that their agency's involvement with supporting religious groups remains relatively stable. Only 19% indicated that the relationship with supporting religious organizations has become *less* significant over the past ten years. Over 35% (n = 28) said that the relationship has become *more* significant, and the greatest number, 39% (n = 51) indicated that the relationship has been relatively stable in its significance. Almost half (48%, n = 38), however, predicted that their relationship with supporting religious groups will become more significant in the coming ten years. Only 14% (n = 11) predict that the relationship will become less significant.

We can conclude, therefore, that whatever its impact may be, the church as a context and support for child welfare services has been and will continue to be influential in the work of these agencies and thus needs to be understood.

Governance

Their church context profoundly effects the governance of these agencies; 60% (47) of the respondents indicated that 76-100% of their board of directors are official representatives of churches and/or other religious organizations. Only 29% (n = 23) indicated that 25% or less of their board members represent their religious constituency; the other 8% (n = 6) ranged between these two extremes.[1]

Budget

As has already been found in the earlier study by Barber (1990), sponsoring religious organizations contribute significant amounts to the budgets of religiously sponsored child welfare agencies. These agencies range in size from those with annual budgets of less than $500,000 to those with annual budgets of more than $5,000,000. No significant relationship was found between the size of the agency budget and the agency's sponsorship (i.e., whether agencies are sponsored partly or entirely by churches and/or religious organizations). Churches and religious organizations directly contribute 28% of these agencies' budgets. In ad-

---

1 Not all statistics add to the full number of respondents, because not all respondents answered every question. Unless the number who did not respond to a particular item on the questionnaire exceeds 5%, this statistic has been considered insignificant and has been omitted in order to simplify discussion of the findings.

dition to the funding from churches and religious organizations, 61 of the agencies receive funding from state and federal grants and contracts, which average 44% of their budgets. Private donations contribute 20% of the budgets to the 61 agencies who receive these donations, and 58 agencies receive endowment income, contributing 21% of their budgets; presumably these private donations and endowment often come from the sponsoring church or religious group's members. When this 41% is added to the 28% contributed directly by churches and religious organizations, 69% of these agencies' budgets can be hypothesized to come from these church-related sources. Although 44 agencies receive client fees, these fees contribute only 10.5% of their budgets. Twenty-seven agencies receive an average of 11.8% of their income from other sources (e.g., income from property, United Way, foundations, estates, and fund raisers).

Staff

The church context has a significant impact on the requirements placed on staff in these agencies. Thirty-six respondents (45.7%) stated that their agencies require their social workers to be Christians. Only 13 (15.6%) require that social workers be members of particular denominations or churches, however, although 15 (19.0%) require church attendance a given percentage of the time. Eight respondents (10.0%) stated other requirements for social workers, including support of the agency's mission as Christian ministry, attendance in the campus church when on duty, modeling Christian behavior, and commitment to Christian faith. On the other hand, 38 (48.1%) stated that none of these religious requirements apply for their social work staff.

Mission, goals, and services of the organization

The clearest impact of the church context on these agencies is in the area of organizational mission and goals. Over two-thirds of the respondents indicated that religious affiliation has a major impact on agency mission and goals, whereas only 6% indicated no impact. An agency's services usually directly reflect its mission and goals, and thus also are influenced by the religious context in which services are offered; over 50% of the respondents indicated at least some impact of the religious context on the nature of services provided by their agencies. Respondents were asked to name programs or services offered by their agencies which, in their assessment, developed because of their agencies' religious context. Respondents most frequently named spiritual life programs ($n = 12$), such as religious education and religious services. Interestingly, many respondents named "typical" child welfare services, such as foster care (n = 10), counseling services (n = 10), residential treatment facilities (n = 10), maternity care and adoption (n = 10), residential group homes (n = 7), emergency shelters (n = 6), homes for developmentally disturbed adults (n = 5), homes for unwed mothers (n = 4), pregnancy counseling (n = 3), family preservation services (n = 3), transitional housing (n = 2), information and referral (n = 1), and in-home services for single parents for two years after delivery (n = 1). Programs listed which may be considered unique to these agencies include pregnancy prevention, parent education, and other family life education programs offered through and for church congregations, as well as with client groups (n = 10); continuing education and support services for professional church workers (n = 2); emergency receiving homes for children whose families are in crisis (n = 2); a project matching church women with pregnant girls for support ("Elizabeth Project") (n = 1); weekday child care consultation to churches (n = 1); a volunteer speakers bureau for churches (n = 1); and a multitude of programs for volunteers (n = 10), including a "friends of children" group, special projects for youth and adult groups from congregations, and summer Bible camps.

Respondents were asked to share their dreams for the future of the agency in its relationship with churches and other religious organizations. These dreams were to include both programs they would like to develop or discontinue and ways to strengthen or weaken ties with churches and religious organizations. By far, the most frequent responses included a desire to increase the support, particularly financial support, of churches and denominations for the work of their agencies (n = 19). The next most frequent response indicated a desire to develop or expand the services of the agency to programs in church congregations and local communities, emphasizing family life education and other preventive and developmental services (n = 16). Seven respondents indicated a desire to develop family counseling and crisis intervention centers in local communities. Six respondents wanted to develop or expand pregnancy, maternity, and adoption programs. Six respondents indicated their desire to work on public relations with church congregations and other local groups. Five respondents wanted to develop or expand the use of volunteers in their agencies. Four respondents expressed a desire to decrease their dependence on government funds. A number of program areas were mentioned as areas for future plans, including foster and group homes (n = 5), day care for poor children (n = 2), treatment of dysfunctional families (n = 1), emergency shelter and residential treatment (n = 1), involving churches in policy advocacy (n = 1), development of a denominationally celebrated Children's Day (n = 1), services to the developmentally disabled (n = 3), alcohol treatment (n = 1), on-campus schools (n = 1), and ties with minority congregations (n = 1).

Summary

For many church-related child welfare agencies, relationships with supporting religious groups give shape to their services. Their governing boards represent the churches and religious groups who support them, and to whom they must report as to use of that support. Their services must be related to the values and mission purposes of the churches on whom they are dependent. By establishing guidelines concerning religious behavior, they attempt to recruit staff who will represent the religious values and beliefs of the supporting religious groups to their clients and communities. Although many of the services of these agencies resemble those of nonsectarian child welfare agencies (emergency shelter, residential child care, foster care, maternity and adoption services, group homes), they often additionally offer or are planning to offer a wide range of community services, often in and through the churches and religious organizations which support them. Such services include family life education and other prevention-oriented family services in congregations and communities, community-based crisis services, involvement of church volunteers in current services and in child advocacy, and even influence in the worship of church communities (i.e., the development of Children's Day worship services). For the most part, agency administrators see the relationship with supporting religious groups as one to be strengthened, not diminished.

Some Guidelines for Church Social Work in Child Welfare Agencies

Given this context and support for the services of these agencies, several guidelines can be posited for social work practice in church-supported child welfare agencies.

1. Develop a theological and Biblical foundation for the church's ministry with children and their families, and firmly anchor services on that foundation.

To the extent that the agency has been founded and/or supported by a church as a response to the church's understanding of its mission, the work of the agency must begin with an understanding of that mission and how the agency can best lead the church in its response to its calling as a faith community. This differs significantly from the context for state and nonsectarian agencies, whose mission springs from the unmet needs of the community and world, to which state agencies are mandated to respond. Although sectarian agencies may offer "standard" child welfare services, (i.e., foster care, residential care, etc.), their underlying mission leads to a rationale and evaluation criteria for services which differ from the rationale and evaluation criteria for similar services offered by public and other private agencies. For example, the rationale for state foster care services begins with the need, i.e., that a given number of children have need of temporary placement because of court decisions, and the state carries responsibility for these children. In contrast, the rationale for a denominational agency's foster care service begins with the mission of the church to receive little ones in the name of Jesus, because to do so is to receive Jesus (Mark 9:37). The church is to lead its people in living the life of service to which we have been called as living witnesses to the lordship of Christ. The church concerns itself with needs after recognizing and responding to the calling of God into service; the needs themselves do not justify service. The varying requirements for religious identification and behavior in the staff employed by the agency can be viewed as an attempt to ensure this fundamental identity with the theology and mission of supporting religious organizations.

Consequently, the church-related child welfare agency must begin with a theological and Biblical foundation for its service. Description of need can then follow as the context of response to God's love and calling into ministry. Presentations to religious groups who support the agency need to begin with an examination of scriptures and theology which calls the church to care for children and their families, not simply with a "proof text" which attempts to tether what the agency is doing to the church community. Otherwise, the church is being asked to respond not out of who it is, but out of what the needs in the world or the services of the agency are, and thus it risks losing its moorings that nurture its service over time in response to changing needs in the world around it.

Jesus' actions and sayings about children were among his most radical and revolutionary. Children were second-class, disposable human beings in the eyes of both the Romans and the Jews in Jesus' world; they were helpless, nonproductive burdens. Although they might survive childhood to become productive and protective of their parents, until then, they were further down the social ladder even than women, the poor, and the lame (Willimon, 1985). When Paul said, "When I was a child, I thought like a child. But when I became a man, I put away childish things (1 Cor. 13:11)," he obviously was not expressing high valuation of childhood and children. Nor did Jesus idealize childhood. His message was, "In my kingdom, *even* helpless, dependent children--the last of all-shall be received" (Mark 9:35-37). In his parable of the last day, Jesus said that some will ask, "Lord, when did we see you hungry, naked, in prison?" And he will respond, "When you did it unto the least of these little ones, these children, you did it unto me" (Matt. 25:31-46). Jesus was saying, "I am the least, the little, the child" (Willimon, 1985). Caring for children, therefore, profoundly expresses our love of Jesus. Beyond the specific sayings about children, the call of Biblical writers in the both Old and New Testaments for justice for the poor and the oppressed provides a powerful foundation for involvement of the church in caring for children and their families in crisis.

Social workers may not be scholarly theologians, but there are resources and persons available, including church leaders in supporting religious organizations, on whom social workers can draw. The church social worker in the child welfare setting can thus articulate a theological and Biblical foundation for services to children and their families that is faithful to the traditions and understandings of a particular church or denomination (see also Garland & Garland, 1990; Garland & Pancoast, 1990; Garland & Parham, forthcoming; Gillogly, 1982; Guy,, 1991; Weber, 1979; and Willimon, 1985).

Once church social workers have firmly anchored services in the church's theology and mission, they can turn the church toward facing the needs of children in their community and the larger world.

2. Keep the relationship between the agency's services and the church's mission prominent in both agency and supporting religious organizations.

The initial establishment and/or support of agency services as expressions of the church's mission must be revisited and emphasized for both agency staff and church members, lest the agency staff begin to view their support simply as another responsibility to be discharged. Church's membership changes over time; child welfare agencies develop new programs and hire new staff. These changes need to be accompanied by a reexamination of the agency's relationship with the faith communities which support and minister through it.

3. Focus the work of the agency around the needs of the church to be involved in ministry, as well as the needs of children and families for services.

To the extent that the role of the church-related child welfare agency is to lead the church in response to the needs of children and families, specialized professional services supported by the church financially may be important but cannot be primary. The discipline for church members of financial support needs to be accompanied by the discipline of personal involvement in ministry with children and families in crisis. The compelling need to involve lay persons in the services of the agency distinguishes the church-related child welfare agency from other agencies perhaps more clearly than any other characteristic of this setting for child welfare services. It also suggests an important niche church-related agencies can fill in the array of a community's child welfare services.

In a sense, social workers employed by churches and their agencies have been commissioned as leaders of the church's ministry to children. As such, our concern needs to be not only marketing our work to churches who are our supporters, but enabling and equipping those supporters to become a part of the work of ministry to and with children and their families. Of course, one of the ways we lead is through providing professional programs that are supported financially by churches. To give financially to support programs for children and families who cannot afford those needed services is a significant way we enable churches to minister. In addition, however, churches and denominations are developing resources and programs through which churches and their members can minister *directly* to children and their families, building on the church's own characteristics as a voluntary association, its own goals and culture, and its voluntary members.

Child welfare services began with volunteers, women in churches who were concerned about orphans and built homes to take them in, volunteers who became advocates for children against physical abuse from families and grinding labor in mines and factories. With the growth of the professions came the growth of professionalized services for children. Gradually, professionals replaced volunteers in providing direct care for children in crisis. Our understanding of how best to serve children in crisis has come almost full circle. We are realizing that as much as children and families in crisis need professional services, what they may need most are volunteers–neighbors and friends who can detect early signs of neglect or abuse; neighbors and friends who can provide needed family supports in times of crisis; loving families willing to become foster, adoptive, and respite families; and friendship, support and mentoring for teenage, single, high-risk parents. The center of energy in our professional field has moved from highly specialized treatment for individual children to family therapy, and now to family preservation and prevention programs. Perhaps the next move is to community programs that involve natural helpers and social networks--the people in our churches–in providing nurturing environments for children and their families, as we have seen in the burgeoning development of grassroots Family Resource Centers (Levine, 1988). There still will be the need for highly specialized treatment services, but these will not be the centerpiece of the church's child welfare services.

4. Provide preventive and developmental services through congregations and religious organizations which reach children and families not "accessible" to other family service agencies.

Church members will often involve themselves in family life education seminars and programs offered by their church; these same church members, however, would never consider seeking out such resources for family living from community agencies, and certainly not through the outpatient educational programs of a hospital. During a typical week, 40% of families attend congregational worship; over 70% of families involve themselves in congregational worship each month. Except for public schools, congregations serve more children and youth, and certainly more parents, than any other institution in our nation (Clark, Fields, & Coleman, 1990). For every child in Sunday school on Sunday morning, 8 children are in church-supported day care centers on Monday; churches provide more day care services than any other institution (Freeman, 1986).

Nevertheless, access to children and families who can benefit from family life education services does not alone justify their provision by the church-related child welfare agency. To proceed only with the justification risks mistaking the church for a satellite family service center or community mental health center rather than relating to its unique mission and role in the lives of families. Practice in this setting, as in the agency itself, needs to be firmly grounded in a theological and Biblical understanding of the nature of family relationships and the role of the church in nurturing health in those relationships.

For Christians, family relationships serve as the most challenging and constant source of discipline in Christian living. The Christian disciplines of love, commitment, self-giving, and forgiveness can be practiced nowhere so readily, although at times with great difficulty, as in family relationships. And these relationships have value beyond the meaning they have for the individuals within them; our family lives are to be a demonstration to those with whom we live and to the world beyond of our discipleship. Jesus said that all will know "that you are my disciples, if you have love for one another" (John 13:35). Our family relationships are to be a witness of God's convenantal love. Thus, the New Testament exhibits concern that nothing be awry in the family life of a Christian (see 1 Thess. 4:3-8; 1 Tim. 3:5, 12; 5:4-8, 14; Titus 2:4-5). The Bible frequently describes the relationship between God and God's people with images from family life; God is bridegroom, husband, suckling mother, and father. God is seen in the love and loyalty and acts of devotion that one expects in family--the response of a father to a child who says, "I'm hungry" (Luke 11:11-13).

The Biblical understanding of the meaning of family life for Christians provides the impetus for family life education for churches. Although many churches may not have overtly identified family life education as a means of spiritual education and discipline for their members, they in fact have implicitly sought to pursue this objective by seeking professionals and media resources that they assume to share their values and beliefs about family life. Despite the vast resources of family professionals and excellent media resources available in many communities, churches often eschew using these, preferring to use resources and leadership from within their own ranks. As an example, James Dobson's family living resources have met with an unparalleled reception by many churches because they are identifiably "Christian." One denominations's parent education program, based clearly and overtly on Biblical principles for family living, has sold over 120,000 copes (*The Family Touch*, 1990).

Church social workers employed in church-related child welfare agencies often find themselves invited to lead congregational family life education programs, because they are seen as both experts and as members of the community of faith. Such opportunities for service provide important linkage between church and agency as well as providing needed resources for the church community. The social worker may well want to use the variety of excellent professional media resources available in conducting family life education and support programs, whether they are overtly Christian or not. They need to be examined and interpreted from the cultural and religious context of the faith community, however, if they are to be congruent with the church's objectives for family life education. Beginning and ending with prayer as the only way in which a family life education program in the church differs from one provided in a community mental health center is like pouring salsa over a chicken pot pie and calling it Mexican food. Instead, the social worker needs to lead church members to examine the values and principles of living implicit throughout programs and media resources in the light of Christian values and beliefs. This makes the service more effective in achieving the church's underlying objectives of spiritual discernment and growth; it also strengthens the relationship between agency and congregation.

5. Use the flexibility of financial support to develop innovative, pilot services not possible in the public sector.

Although no agency has enough money to address all the needs presented to it, nor even to do well all it has purposed to do, church-related agencies do not carry the responsibility for meeting the needs of all children in the same manner as state agencies. The purpose of the church and her agencies and membership is not to provide for the social and welfare needs of a society which its government has been negligent to address. The church is not and cannot be reduced to a stop-gap social service agency. Sometimes, churches and their agencies can speak out for social justice from their position of relative independence from government support when those in public agencies do not have the leverage to do so. Church social workers can be prophetic voices, leading the church in challenging society's social injustices, not assuming that the church's only role is to minister to those who have been run over by those injustices.

> Private charity can never be an adequate substitute for public justice. Yet our national rhetoric has been that it is proper for government to subsidize three-martini corporate lunches but improper for government to subsidize child care to help millions of poor working mothers escape welfare; that spending millions of dollars on golf outings and sports tickets and barber shops for defense contractors is a more justifiable national security than teaching poor children to read, write, and compute; that more government support for rich families strengthens them; while more government help for poor families weakens them; that a child's right to life ends at birth and does not include the right to adequate prenatal and nutritional care before birth or survival health, housing, and family supports after birth? (Edelman, 1987, pp. 36-37).

One of the responsibilities of the church agency, then, is to be an advocate–a prophet speaking out against oppression, including the oppression of dependent children whose needs are not being addressed effectively. At times, that means involving the agency and its supporting religious organizations in political advocacy in ways that public agencies find difficult or impossible. Another form of advocacy, however, is the development of innovative, pilot programs designed to research the possibilities of more effective, caring programs for children and their families. Because many church-related agencies do not rely solely on fees-per-service formulas, but instead have some limited flexibility as a consequence of donations and endowment, they can develop such pilot projects.

6. Evaluate services using criteria sensitive not only to the expectations of professional practice but also to the mission and goals of the supporting religious organizations.

Public and private non-sectarian social service agencies often emphasize time-limited, outcome focused goals and the relative effectiveness of services in reaching these goals. They design services to help clients to get on with their lives beyond the social service agency. Although such evaluation is obviously important to them, church-related agencies may also have goals which emphasize the development of personal relationships, mutual support, and systems through which members and the group as a whole can live as a community and pursue their shared mission. Churches may be particularly interested in the extent to which clients are integrated into the life of a church community as a consequence of service--the extent to which they are "evangelized." Services designed to prevent problems and enhance the development of persons and their families and communities may be more easily accepted, even when outcome is more difficult to prove, than in a more professionalized social service context. On the other hand, highly professionalized services offered in a confidential setting are less familiar in the *modus operandi* of a church community.

In addition to these subtle but significant differences in the expected client outcomes for church-related agencies when compared with public agencies, church-related agencies need to consider ways they can evaluate the effectiveness of their leadership in the mission of the church. For example, the church-related agency may need to include as part of its evaluation the numbers and extent to which lay persons have been involved in the financial support and actual services provided by the agency, and the consequence of that involvement for the lay persons and their churches.

Finally, the church-related agency needs to evaluate the consequences of its inevitable choices concerning the use of its limited resources in the face of almost limitless possibilities for service. What does the choice to offer expensive residential treatment and treatment foster home cost in terms of other services–such as church-based prevention and family support programs–which could not be implemented? What inadvertent positive consequences did the agency's leadership in a congregation-based child advocacy program have for the financial support forthcoming from that congregation for services to seriously emotionally disturbed children?

What are the advantages and costs incurred when a formerly centralized staff is dispersed to community-based centers?

The Future of Church-Related Child Welfare Services: Illustrative Services and Programs

The church-related agency has access to potential networks of community social support that can become a part of the resources for client families served by residential care, foster care, group homes, and adoption programs. Church-related agencies are uniquely situated to provide, therefore, those services that coordinate the direct professional care needed by a child and the child's family with nonprofessional–but just as critical–support, nurture and connection in a community.

Volunteers in Residential Care Agencies

Church volunteers can be a critical resource in providing care for children who have no family to whom they can return, and who may not be adoptable or currently appropriate for foster home placement. These children still very much need relationships with caring adults in a world beyond the residential child care facility, adults who care for them not because they are paid to care, but because they have chosen to care. Some children need these relationships to be ongoing but intensive. Others may evolve over time into consideration of foster care or even adoption, although this is not initially a stated goal. For others, friendship that will last into the adult years after release from agency care meets a critical need. The preparation, training, care in matching volunteer with child, and ongoing support and consultation for these volunteers requires professional expertise and ongoing involvement no less demanding than professional therapeutic services offered directly to families.

Therapeutic Foster Care

Foster parents are often recruited from churches; they bring a special strength to their work out of their sense of Christian calling and commitment. Religious fervor can also lead persons to volunteer as foster parents or in other roles related to the agency who have neither the personal strengths, knowledge of their own strengths and limitations, or skills for the demanding work of loving a child in crisis and, even harder, their families. The social worker has the sensitive task of screening volunteers and finding the most effective ways they can be involved and can experience the spiritual growth that comes as a consequence of disciplined Christian service.

The social worker can work with the foster parents' church, helping them to become of a system of support and extended family for the foster family. The development of such a support system often does not happen naturally. It requires the subtle, highly intricate work of a professional who knows how to intervene in and strengthen natural systems of support (Garland & Pancoast, 1990). It may require recruitment, education, and ongoing consultation with concerned persons in the church community–the pastor, youth minister, Sunday School teachers, church basketball coach, and persons willing to provide respite care for the foster parents. Finally, therapeutic foster care may need the agency to serve as a 24 hour consultation resource and source of regular respite care for the child and the foster parents.

In-home Crisis Program

State child welfare agencies are increasingly offering in-home crisis intervention programs. These programs aim to prevent out of home placement, intervening for a short time with many hours of professional involvement in the home to prevent out-of-home placement. A social worker may be in the home providing family life education services, family therapy, and making community connections and referrals with a family for over 20 hours per week, carrying only two families in their caseload at a time (Whittaker, Kinney, Tracy, & Booth, 1990). The Homebuilder's program, for example, has had a phenomenal success rate–88% of the families served are still intact one year after termination of services; at the time of referral, these families were on the brink of one or more children being placed outside the family. Social workers in this program carry a caseload of 2-5 families, with 8-25 hours of direct services with each family weekly for a maximum of three months. They average 8.3 hours per week with each family for four weeks (*Protecting Children*, 1987).

Church agencies can bring resources to such programs which are not available to the social worker from a public agency. Church members can be involved directly as volunteers with the family in crisis–providing transportation, offering friendship to parents and children, providing respite care, and offering volunteer professional consultation from church members (lawyers, physicians, car mechanics, etc.) A Texas child protection agency, for example, established a program in which church groups adopt a child protection worker (Duncan, Myers, Davies, & Casey, 1988). This worker calls on the designated group for a myriad of supports when working with an isolated family who needs to experience a supportive network of relationships. The evaluation of the program indicates that the major drawback has been that the social workers did not understand the church networks well enough to avail themselves of intangible resources like befriending and other forms of social support. Church agencies may be able to develop these relationships more effectively if their staff understand the church community and its strengths and limitations.

Of course, these program initiatives take enormous amounts of time with church groups and individual church staff members and volunteers, as well as with clients. This time is not readily recorded as units of service and is not likely to be third party reimbursable. For this reason, church agencies may be able to take initiative in these programs and develop demonstration projects not possible in state agencies.

Church-related agencies offering these kinds of services have moved away from providing services exclusively on the children's home campus or within the agency. Instead, they provide services through the congregations and religious groups in their local communities. The agency also becomes a source of consultation for churches and religious groups who want to provide ministries to children and their families who need services, even though they may not be at risk for out-of-home placement.

Providing Consultation to Churches and Religious Groups

Social workers can help churches identify their resources and needs for ministry, the needs of children and families in their communities, and the ways in which churches can respond to those needs. For example, ChildServ, a church-related child welfare agency in Chicago, helps churches conduct assessments of the needs of children in their communities and of the resources they have to respond to those needs. They work with churches in focusing their efforts, developing new services, and evaluating those services. Consultants from ChildServ usually work with churches between nine and eighteen months, in many respects as a church staff member loaned to the church for a contracted period of time. Consultants have helped churches develop child care services, child abuse prevention programs, teen pregnancy programs, and alternative programs for youth at risk for gang involvement (Friedrich, 1990). Consultation may involve making guest presentations in churches and religious groups, ranging from preaching Sunday morning sermons to leading workshops and retreats. Consultants may offer assistance in program development and/or management, such as program planning and maintenance, training and consulting with volunteers, or developing evaluative methods that are congruent with the church's objectives in ministry.

Congregational consultation involves an investment of financial resources and additional staff time on the part of the agency. In addition to the projected outcomes of the consultation projects themselves, however, such consultation services have two other positive outcomes for the agency. First, it keeps agency staff involved in supporting churches and religious groups, thus nurturing the mutual commitment of these organizations. Churches now have social work faces and personal relationships to identify with the agency; they may well, therefore, be more supportive of other work of the agency. Second, professional staff who work primarily with troubled children and dysfunctional families may find working in prevention programs and developing community support services a way to retain their perspective on the place of their work in the larger fabric of the church's ministry with children and families and a gratifying and welcome respite from their usual responsibilities. Such experiences may provide protection from burn-out and thus reduce staff turnover.

Examples of programs for which agency staff can provide consultation to churches and religious organizations include:

Day care. One of the most critical needs of families, particularly low-income families. is affordable, quality day care. Currently, churches are the primary providers of such care; one church in three now houses a child care program. Churches house at least one-third of the child care programs in the United States. For every child in Sunday School on Sunday, eight children are in church-housed child care on Monday; 2.3 million children receive day care from our nation's churches (Freeman, 1986). With the resources of excellent facilities that otherwise would be idle for much of the week, and the ready accessibility in community neighborhoods, many churches are providing this ministry to families.

Church-related child welfare agencies can help churches shape these ministries to respond to those with the greatest needs. For example, sliding fee scales can help poor families receive care for their children not affordable in the private for-profit sector of the child care business. Many churches offer Mother's Day Out and other respite programs which can be modified to serve, in addition to those parents who seek out such support, isolated parents who are at-risk for abusing and neglecting their children, or parents whose children have special needs for whom respite care is a critical support.

Volunteer and paid staff in such programs need training in the skills and sensitivity necessary to reach out with encouragement and nurture for these parents and their children. These services can be combined with parent education and support groups, volunteer family visitors trained in befriending and supporting isolated parents who may be un-skilled in developing and maintaining social relationships, and a profes-sional social worker available for crisis intervention and referral networks with community services. For example, the Soulard Family Center in the inner city of St. Louis, Missouri, provides drop-in child care services for children and personal support services for their parents. No fee is charged for services, but for every three times a child is left at the Center, the parents are required to participate in an enrichment or support activity for parents which is offered by the Center (Preventing abuse before it starts, 1990).

Friendly visiting. One church in the Chicago area brings baskets of needed baby items to new mothers in the hospital who have been iden-tified by social services staff as "high risk," such as single teenage parents. The baskets include a "certificate" for one evening of in-home child care by one of the women in the church and the offer of continued suppor-tive friendship, a monthly visit in which the church woman includes mother and baby in game-like activities that support the baby's develop-ment, and on-loan toys for the new baby and mother to play with together. Services such as these can be particularly significantly when linked with a drop-in family resource center, crisis intervention services, and parent support groups.

"Phone Friends." Another church has developed a telephone reas-surance network of latchkey kids and senior citizens. The "phone friends" not only talk to one another each afternoon after school, but meet some days of the week at the church for special activities.

Parent to Parent Programs. Parents of emotionally disturbed, physi-cally ill, and developmentally handicapped children and adult children often gain enormous support and new skills and information that help them cope with their family's situation simply by meeting and spending time with other parents who face similar challenges. Such a network of support, when coupled with professional services of family counseling and respite care available from the agency, can enable some families to continue to provide daily care who would otherwise be forced to con-sider placement outside the home.

Ministries with the families of prisoners. Some church volunteers provide friendship, transportation, emotional support, linkage with other resources, and advocacy in behalf of families of incarcerated persons through church prison ministries (Garland, 1985b). This can be par-ticularly critical support for dependent children whose mothers are im-prisoned. Churches who have been involved in providing worship services and visiting in jails and prisons often welcome consultation designed to extend their ministry to families.

Child advocacy. Children are the poorest group in our nation. Although the U.S. remains the world's wealthiest nation, its infant mortality rate ranks 20th in the world, roughly comparable to that of Hong Kong. Infant mortality is twice as high for blacks as for whites. One out of four women now carrying children will not receive any prenatal care before the births of their babies, resulting in higher rates of mortality, low birth weight, physical defects, and illness. Half of the children in this country younger than 15 have never visited a dentist. Two out of 5 children are not immunized against childhood diseases (Children's Defense Fund, 1990; and Zigler & Gilman, 1990).

These statistics represent only a small part of the data we have to show that our nation is guilty of child neglect. When church groups are confronted with this information, the first response is often, "I had no idea," and the second is, "What can we do?" The United Methodists waged a "Campaign for Children," involving United Methodist women's groups all across the nation in a variety of advocacy efforts locally and nationally in behalf of children, ranging from developing tutoring programs in inner-city schools to writing letters to state and national legislators (Guy & Smith, 1988).

Agency staff can bring these concerns to the attention of church groups and help them to find ways to act in behalf of children. A number of denominations have developed national child advocacy task forces; the National Council of Churches provides a forum for those concerned about child advocacy. Agency staff can draw on the excellent publications and newsletters of the Children's Defense Fund for the information about children's needs both locally and nationally, and for resources in guiding the church's advocacy for children (Children's Defense Fund, 1983, 1990; Guy, 1991; see also *Family Resource Coalition Report,* Freeman, 1986; Garland & Parham, forthcoming; Kelker, 1987; United Voices for Children, 1980.)

Summary

The nuns in New Orleans and the Baptist women in Louisville had a clear vision of what needed to happen; children orphaned by wars needed shelter and care, and the people of God needed to respond. The situation facing church-related child welfare agencies seems much more complex. Our resources of money and staff seem so limited in the face of a whole array of complex needs. What churches often want to give–a party for "orphans" on a holiday, or used clothing and toys–do not fit the needs of the very troubled children and families whom we serve. Effective social workers in a church-related agency need far more than skills in family therapy with troubled children and their families; they need to be *students of theology and the Bible* who can firmly root what they do to the values and mission of the church community, *fervent speakers* who can help churches understand the needs and their role in responding to those needs, *visionaries* who can look at the church's resources and the needs of children and families and bring them together in creative new services, *program planners and implementers* who understand the strengths and limitations of the church as a voluntary religious organization, and *consultants* who can train and support lay persons in key roles in the lives of children and their families. Thank God that the power and indwelling Spirit the Ursuline nuns had to undergird their work is the same power and Spirit on which we can draw in the work before us.

REFRENCES

Barber, Cyril A. (1990). Residential care quiz produces surprising results. *Caring,* 6 (1), 25-26.

Blackburn, Bill, and Blackburn, Deana Mattingly (1987). *Caring in times of family crisis*. Nashville: Southern Baptist Convention Press.

Carlson, Rick (1980). *A handbook for the child advocate.* Chicago: United Methodists, Northern Illinois Conference.

Children's Defense Fund (1983). *In celebration of children: An interfaith religious action kit*. Washington, D.C.: Children's Defense Fund.

Children's Defense Fund (1990). *Children 1990: A report card, briefing book, and action primer.* Washington, D.C.: Children's Defense Fund.

Clark, Merrell, Fields, Carl, and Coleman, Ora (1990). *Congregations, parenting, and the prevention of delinquency*, as quoted in *Mission possible: Churches supporting fragile families* (1990). National Crime Prevention Council, 1700 K Street, NW, Washington, D.C., 20007.

Duncan, D., Myers, E., Davies, D. R.,, and Casey, D. E. (1988). *Adopting child protection workers: A new response by the religious community to the crisis of child abuse and neglect.* Texas Department of Human Services, 701 W. 51st St., P. O. Box 2960 M.C. 537-W, Austin, TX 78769.

Edelman, Marian W. (1987). *Families in peril: An agenda for social change.* Cambridge: Harvard University Press.

Ewers, Duane A. (1983). *A ministry of caring.* Participant's workbook and Leader's guide. Discipleship Resources, P.O. Box 840, Nashville, TN 37202.

Family Resource Coalition Report. Published three times a year by Family Resource Coalition, Suite 1625, 230 Michigan Avenue, Chicago, IL 60601. (phone: 312-726-4750).

The Family Touch (1990). Parenting by Grace/Covenant Marriage goes to the Bahamas. *The Family Touch: Family Enrichment News and Views,* Fall 1990. (a newsletter published by the Family Enrichment Section of the Baptist Sunday School Board, 127 Ninth Avenue North, Nashville, TN 37234.)

Freeman, Margery (Ed.) (1986). *Called to act: Stories of child care advocacy in our churches.* Child Advocacy Office, Division of Church and Society, National Council of the Churches of Christ in the U.S.A., 475 Riverside Dr., Rm. 572, New York, NY 10115.

Friedrich, Laura Dean (1990). Serving children and families through agency consultation with local churches. In D. Garland and D. Pancoast (Eds.) *Churches ministering with families.* Irving, TX: Word.

Garland, Diana R. (1985a). Family life education, family ministry, and church social work: Suggested relationships. *Social Work and Christianity,* 12, 14-26.

Garland, Diana R. (1985b). Volunteer ministry to families of prisoners and the Christian social worker's role. *Social Work and Christianity,* 12, 13-25.

Garland, Diana (1986). Christians in social work, Christian social ministry, and church social work: Necessary distinctions. *Social Work and Christianity,* 13, 18-25.

Garland, Diana R. (1990). Parent networks: Programs for empowering parents. In Garland, D.S.R., and Pancoast, D. (Eds.) *Churches ministering with families.* Irving, TX: Word.

Garland, Diana R., and Chapman, Katherine (forthcoming). *Self-esteem: Parenting by grace.* Nashville: Family Ministry Department, The Sunday School Board of the Southern Baptist Convention.

Garland, D.E., and Garland D.S.R. (1990). The family: Biblical and theological perspectives. In Christian D. Kettler and Todd H. Speidell (Eds.), *Incarnational ministry: The presence of Christ in church, society, and family.* Colorado Springs: Helmers and Howard.

Garland, Diana R., and Pancoast, Diane L. (Eds.) (1990). *Churches ministering with families.* Irving, TX: Word.

Garland, Diana R., and Parham, Robert (forthcoming). *Precious in His eyes: Welcoming the children*. Birmingham: New Hope.

Gillogly, Robert R. (1982). *Sacred Shelters: Church-related children's homes*. The Villages, Inc., Box 1695, Topeka, KS 66601.

Guy, Kathleen (1991). *Welcome the children*. Washington, D.C.: Children's Defense Fund.

Guy, Kathleen, and Smith, Chiquita G. (1988). *Campaign for children*. Women's Division, General Board of Global Ministries, The United Methodist Church, 7820 Reading Road, Caller No. 1800, Cincinnati, OH 45222-1800.

Johns, Mary Lee (1988). *Developing church programs to prevent child abuse*. Austin: Texas Conference of Churches.

Johnson, Ronald, and Long, Russell (1983). *Social Ministry: A congregational manual*. Philadelphia: Parish Life Press, 2900 Queen Lane, Philadelphia, PA 19129.

Kelker, K.A. (1987). *Making the system work: An advocacy workshop for parents*. Families as Allies Project, Regional Research Institute for Human Services, Portland State University, Portland, OR 97207-0751.

Larson, Jim (1984). *Strengthening families: A church guide*. Commission on Family Ministries and Human Sexuality, Office of Education for Christian Life and Ministry, National Council of the Churches of Christ in the U.S.A., 475 Riverside Dr., Room 708, New York, NY 10115-0050.

Levine, Carole (Ed.) (1988). *Programs to strengthen families: A resource guide*. Chicago: The Family Resource Coalition.

Nichol, Harry (1983). The missing ingredient was people ministering to people. *Lake Bluff/Chicago Homes for Children News*, 4 (2), 5.

Parent Education Ministry. Archdiocese of New York, Office of Christian and Family Development. 203 Sand Lane, Staten Island, NY 10305.

Patterson, S. C. (1988) For children's sake. *The Interpreter*. September 22-29.

Preventing abuse before it starts (1990). *Ecumenical Child Care Newsletter*, 8 (6, November/December), 2.

Protecting Children (1987). Summer issue, pp. 12-13.

Spressart, Janet Furness (1988). The vulnerable Christian social worker: "Wise as serpents and harmless as doves." *Social Work and Christianity*, 15, 44-54.

United Church Board for Homeland Ministries. *The family album: Resources for family life ministries*. United Church of Christ, 1400 North Seventh St., St. Louis, MO 63106.

United Voices for Children (1980). *A handbook for the child advocate.* United Voices for Children, 1661 N. Northwest Highway, Park Ridge, Illinois 60068.

Wallach, Lorraine B., and Weissbourd, Bernice (1979). *Creating drop-in centers: The Family Focus model.* Family Focus, Inc., 2300 Green Bay road, Evanston, IL 60201.

Weber, Hans Ruedi (1979). *Jesus and the children: Biblical resources for study and preaching.* Atlanta: John Knox Press.

Whittaker, James K. (1971). Colonial child care institutions: Our heritage of care. *Child Welfare*, 50, 396-400.

Whittaker, James K., Kinney, Jill, Tracy, Elizabeth M., and Booth, Charlotte (Eds.) (1990). *Reaching high-risk families: Intensive family preservation in human services.* Hawthorne, NY: Aldine de Gruyter.

Willimon, William (1985). Receiving little Jesus. *Christian Century*, December 4, 1985, 1109-1110.

Zigler, Edward F., and Gilman, Elizabeth P. (1990). An agenda for the 1990s: Supporting families. In David Blankenhorn, Steven Bayme, and Jean Bethke Elshtain (Eds.). *Rebuilding the nest: A new commitment to the American family.* Milwaukee: Family Service America.

Chapter 6

Social Work Practice in an International Context

by Donoso S. Escobar*

In South Africa, we have apartheid churches: only the White Church is the real Church. The Black churches became mission fields. There was an African Church, a Coloured Church, an Indian Church. Their presidents were elected by Whites in their conference, and then they appointed a missions director, who chairs the meetings of the other churches . . . In those days the Bantustans had commissioners appointed by the government, and likewise churches had superintendents appointed by the White churches. And so an apartheid context creates an apartheid church (Frank Chikane (1990), General Secretary of the South African Council of churches).

The religious presence of Jesus of Nazareth in the Jewish society of his times linked orthodoxy with orthopraxy: applied theology. It was precisely his commitment to applied theology that eventually placed him in the hands of the religious authorities advocating his execution. The dialectical quest had been delineated over 700 years before by the Hebrew prophet Isaiah. Isaiah implied that servanthood and political power, oppression and liberation, social injustice and God's salvation were mutually exclusive social acts (Isa. 52 and 53). When Jesus claimed to be the fulfilment of Isaiah's prophecy, he declared himself as the deliverer of the oppressed (Lk. 4:16-19). Later in his teachings, Jesus instilled this commitment in those followers who constituted the church (Matt. 5), thus making his church responsible for a social action intensive agenda.

To discuss church from a social work perspective is to focus on the holistic character of its task. Basic to this task is the need to conceptualize church as part of society, not detached from it. The church's purpose can be accomplished only within its social environment. From a social work perspective, church must therefore be understood as an integral

*Donoso S. Escobar is Associate Professor of Social Work, Carver School of Church Social Work, The Southern Baptist Theological Seminary. Before joining the seminary faculty in 1983, he served as Director of the Immigration and Refugee Service, Home Mission Board, Southern Baptist Convention.

part of its community. This is another way to propose that church as a social actor is a subsystem of the larger system of society and, ultimately, of the rest of creation. The interwoven relationship of church and the rest of humanity is implied in Jesus's prayer asking the Father not that the church be removed from the world, but that it be kept from evil (Jn. 17:15).

From systems theory, social workers have learned to appreciate the difference between open systems and closed systems. Closed systems are characterized by impermeable boundaries; this rigidity propels systems toward self-destruction. On the other hand, ability to exchange energy with their environments permits open systems to cope with change and to remain healthy.[1] Transactions between church and the non-church sector of society result in a healthy exchange of energy which benefits both members and non-members, the church and the "un-churched." Addressing the church, Jesus gave little merit to the practice of doing good to those that reciprocate in kind, to giving only to those who are able to repay, or to loving only those who are willing to respond in love (Mat. 5:38-48). The ultimate exhortation and perhaps the most painful command given by Jesus to the church was: Love your enemies. In Jesus' paradigm, Christians become better Christians not only when they interact with other Christians but when they interact with non-Christians and, by extension, with the rest of God's creation. In this regard, biblical metaphors referring to the church are very revealing: vine (Jn. 5), growing to produce fruits that someone else might enjoy; *salt of the earth* (Mat. 5:13), intended to preserve what is perishable; *building under construction* (I Cor. 3:9), where the interdependence of each stone is critical, but its position irrelevant in terms of importance (Eph. 2:20-22).

Viewing the church as an integral part of the community at large allows one to expect that both members and clergy are obliged to promote and participate in the well-being of society. From Jesus' perspective, the church is an instrument which facilitates God's interaction with humanity.[2] Again, from a systems' perspective, what affects the community at large must affect the community of faith (church, that is) even if church chooses to ignore it or deny it. The church's task, then, acquires an ecosystemic character: church becomes a matrix of interpersonal networks (Garland, 1988). This ecosystemic character of the church makes it humanly relevant in three areas: (1) historically, (2) culturally, and (3) sociologically. When considering the historical relevance of the church, one focuses on the time and space dimension; cultural relevance focuses on the instrumental dimension of the church. The concept of social relevance stresses the integrative dimension of the church. This tridimensional view provides the basis for church social work intervention that transcends geographical and political boundaries. The model is illustrated by the diagram below.

A Social Work Perspective of the Church's Task
A model for Practice

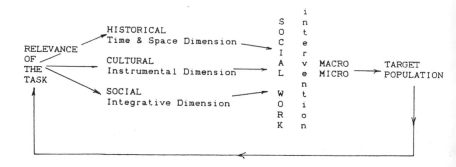

Historical Relevance: Time and Space Dimension
of the Church

The church as designed by Jesus was intended to respond in the here-and-now[3] until "the end of the world" (Mat. 28:20, *KJV*). Because the church was to develop amidst a hostile political and religious environment, fear and disappointment would be overcome by the assured presence of Jesus.

The metaphysical presence of Jesus in the church (Mat. 28:20), however, was contingent upon the church's involvement in the "witnessing" process. Witnessing was interpreted by New Testament writers as the tangible expression of faith: praxis[4] in the world around them. James linked faith and works to the issue of social justice. This New-testamentarian view of church-in-environment is familiar to social workers, whose code of ethics bind them to promote social justice,[5] even within their own organizational settings. One may argue that when the church has focused on its own organizational welfare, it has tended to neglect the plight of the oppressed.[6] Gutierrez (1973) has raised the issue in the theological field:

> Because the Church has inherited its structures and its life-style from the past, it finds itself today somewhat out of step with the history which confronts it. But what is called for is not simply a renewal and adaptation of pastoral methods. It is

rather a question of a new ecclesial consciousness and a redefinition of the task of the Church in a world in which it is not only *present*, but of which it *forms a part* more than it suspected in the past. In this new consciousness and redefinition, intraecclesial problems take a second place (p. 143).

Functioning internationally, the church has encountered three temptations with three paralyzing consequences which negate the *here-and-nowness* of the church: (1) denominationalism, which brings about partisanism; (2) self-aggrandizment, which fosters colonialism and, (3) political compromise, which results in a state religion.

Denominationalism

When the church is motivated by denominationalism, it tends to adopt a transitional corporation model. Programatic decisions are made by distant foreign mission boards which have no meaningful representation of the target population; the human misery of marginal groups becomes raw material for promotional pieces; and the number of "souls" converted to the denomination becomes the measure of success. The church brings to the host country its own exclusive imported leadership which controls and dispenses the denominational resources available to the "locals." Social workers serving overseas find their work compromised by commitment to their own technologies and cultural-religious values vis a vis the need for an indigenous social work agenda in the host country (Roan, 1980; Quiroz-Martin, 1986; Patel, 1987; Escobar, 1988). Social workers in church-related settings overseas then may find themselves attempting to harmonize denominational expectations, local need, and their own standards of professional performance.[7]

Self-Aggrandizement

Self-aggrandizement as a motivational force is manifested in an attitude of *Mater et Magistra*[8] from the part of the church where church sponsored programs must conform to patterns established by the sponsoring church or denomination. The practical manifestations of this mentality may be best appreciated in the presence of imported educational materials, translated church songs, and imported liturgy and methods. In the fashion of industrial vertical integration,[9] the church brings to the host country its own designed and produced programs, materials and, literally, its own music, with no regard for the difference in cultural contexts. For example, a brief perusal of the *Himnario Bautista* (1978) (Baptist Song Book) utilized by many churches in Latin America reveals,(1) only ten percent of the tunes have a Hispanic origin, and (2) only ten percent of the composers have Hispanic surnames. The Lutheran church Spanish song book, *Culto Cristiano,* offers a liturgy characterized by "a strong influence of Lutheran reform. Most of it has been taken directly from the first original German liturgies, although music of Anglican or Roman origin has been used" (p. viii).

Church social workers unfamiliar with the complexities of international practice need to avoid the trap of professional self-sufficiency and an exclusive Westernized practice. For example, a church social worker doing family therapy in a Laotian village where polygamous marriages are acceptable.[10] A systemic view of church would remind workers in church-related agencies that church as a system is in a constant becoming. This is consistent with Jesus' expression of continuing action: ". . . I shall build my church" (Matt. 16:18). The becoming church actively exchanges energy with its community. Making the church's facilities available for community activities would only be a beginning.

Political Compromise

Political compromise is perhaps one of the most pervasive dangers that the church has encountered throughout its existence (Boff, 1989, p. 9). Self-preservation could be argued as the reason, but is it a valid reason? Certainly, the church has a task and thus needs to survive. Nevertheless, the church's task is not to perpetuate its own existence, particularly by compromising its calling. Subjection to state authority, based on an interpretation of Romans 13:1-7, has been argued; but this position has been challenged since Nazi Germany (Yoder, 1972). Political compromise voids the prophetic call of the church. By selectively supporting the agenda of the ruling party, the church becomes an instrument for political manipulation.[11]

The current dismantling of the Lenninist system in the Soviet Union, the fiasco of military solutions in Central America, the current civil rights violations throughout the Middle East, Africa and Asia, and the pervasiveness of institutionalized discrimination in the United States of America indicate that the human race is yet to design an oppression-free political system. Meanwhile, a historically relevant church has the task of denouncing injustice, announcing a better options and portraying those options in its daily transactions, whatever the cost to itself. Social workers bound to denominations who are politically compromised face what Cnaan (1988) calls contradiction between ideology and practice, Cnaan reminds social workers of the discriminatory nature of professional practice when such a compromise has been made.

Denominational strategists have linked the cultural relevance of the church to outreach efforts. In 1982, Oscar Romo, of the Southern Baptist Convention, challenged his staff toward "packing the message of Christ in the most culturally attractive way." One may agree with Romo only to a point. The difficulty lies over the marketing model idea. It can be argued that Jesus wanted not to market his good news to the poor but to promote justice and good will among humans. Jesus was interested in the sharing of the abundance of God's grace with others. When the multitudes were convinced of his religious and political charisma, Jesus chose solitude (Jn. 6:1-15); he was willing to sacrifice popularity if the case so required (Jn. 6:60-67). Jesus' ultimate instructions given to the church, "You shall be my witness in Jerusalem, in all Judea, and Samaria and to the ends of the earth (Acts 1:8), underscored the instrumentality of the church in a crosscultural world. The concept of instrumentality of the church is consistent with a systemic interpretation of its nature: In the ecosystem of creation there is a role for the church.

Viewing the church from a perspective of cultural relevancy has at least three major implications for international church social work practice:(1) it fosters a rediscovery of the term "service"; (2) it suggests the need for a redefinition of spirituality; and (3) it underscores the humanness of the church.

Rediscovering Service (Ministry)

The Greek term DIAKONEO used in the New Testament is a translation of the verb "to serve" or "to minister," from which the English word deacon originates. It implies that where human need exists, there is someone willing to satisfy that need. The Greek noun DIAKONIA, the act of ministering, presupposes commitment to alleviating someone else's need. Jesus stated clearly that his mission was not to be served (DIAKONETHENAI) but to serve (DIAKONESAI) (Matt. 20:28). His expectations were that at the end of history the church would have faithfully served him not by having ministered to itself, but through having served the socially marginalized masses (Matthew 25:44-46). From an ecosystemic view, the role of the church is to provide service to those who remain programatically neglected by welfare bureaucracies. This commitment to the poor has been addressed by unconventional theologians who have ventured to question the cultural relevance of the church in reference to the poor and the socially marginalized (Gutierrez, 1988; Alves, 1984; Comblin, 1979; Dussel, 1978; Tamez, 1982; Boesak, 1977; 1984; Tutu, 1984; Shorter, 1977; Webster, 1982).

The social work profession is rooted in the idea of public service. In fact, once upon a time, professional social workers were committed to public service.[12] Whatever the reasons are behind the trend toward privatization of practice, the fact remains that social work pristine values are embedded solidly with service to the socially marginalized.

Redefining Spirituality

Social workers have begun to discover the concept of spirituality as a unit of analysis. Not only are social work scholars acknowledging the reality of spirituality but they are linking it to the well being of people.[13] How does one develop spirituality in an affluent society? How is spirituality developed in the context of social marginality? Is Western Christianity conducive to the enhancement of spirituality for Third World populations? How? Under what circumstances? How does the spirituality of the worker impact the therapeutic relationship? How does the spiritual journey of a developing nation affect its social welfare policies? These are research questions that need to be field tested by church social workers in international settings for practice. Peruvian theologian Gustavo Gutierrez (1985) has suggested that spiritual childhood is a prerequisite for commitment to the poor. Out of professional commitment, church social workers have the opportunity to invite the church to a journey with the needy. This journey which will imply descending from the podium of *Mater et Magistra* to reflect on the church's own spirituality as it walks along with the homeless, the unskilled physically impaired, the street child, the hungry, the mentally ill–in essence, with the rejected ones of society.

Such a journey will make evident the level of humanness of the church: its capacity for empathy, genuiness, and respect. Church social workers could facilitate the church's journey toward humanness precisely by shaping the church's task within the framework of social work ministries. This is possible because church social work practice with the socially marginalized dramatizes God's initiative toward the oppressed in the person of Jesus. Jesus identifies with suffering unto death and God elevates the poor of the land to the status of owners of God's reign (Mat. 5:3).

Underscoring Humanness

Humanization of the church is central in a parable told by Jesus during a social occasion. The parable has to do with a banquet offered by a wealthy person. Because of the absence of the original guests, the servants were ordered to "bring in the poor, the crippled, the blind and the lame." In a society which identified these people as punished by God, the lesson was essentially blasphemous. However, one of the truths Jesus intended to convey to his church was that it was the will of God for the servant church to descend from a position of social and political influence and go to the crossroads of life where human suffering abounds. This is the church's movement toward humanization.

Social Relevance: The Integrative Dimension of the Church

The social relevance of the church is rooted in the doctrine of the incarnation, the Christian belief that Jesus is God incarnate. The prologue of the Fourth Gospel in the New Testament suggests that from the moment the *Logos* (Christ Jesus, God incarnate) became flesh, a new set of transactions was initiated between Creator and creatures . . . those "who received him," John says, became sons and daughters of God. For John, the unbeliever becomes a believer only after being exposed to the touch of the *Logos* made flesh, after having been exposed to the *Logos'* personhood. Those who willingly accept the *Logos'* relationship develop a new world view, one that fosters sisterhood and brotherhood among humans: A new social order is established. In this new social order, runaway slaves returning to their masters were no longer to be viewed as slaves, they were to be received as a brother or a sister. They were expected to be treated with the same courtesy and social dispensations that their master would grant to the pastor of the church (Philem.). Individuals of different ethnic backgrounds were to be granted the opportunity of full membership (Acts 8:26-40). When a pastor questioned the wisdom of accepting socially excludable non-jews into the community of faith, the pastor was exhorted not to "call unclean what God has made clean" (Acts 10). A divorced woman whose questionable past and ethnic background made her socially unworthy was appointed missionary to the Samaritans (Jn. 4).

These and other radical practices were part of the utopic quest of Jesus and his church. They were radical when compared to the religious system of Jesus' times, a system dominated by orthodoxy but devoid of orthopraxy. The new order would reconcile both. In terms of social work's contribution to a better society, Neuhous (1977) has said:

> The vision of public policy is of a better society in a far from the best of all possible worlds. In Christ we participate in an eternal life that transcends what is usually meant by the political task of history. This transcendence can be, but need not be,

a distraction from the political task. Rather, we take the human enterprise and its politics more seriously because we recognize the eternal significance human life has been given by God (p. 59).

Again, by professional commitment, social workers in a church setting may claim the intentionality of the Christian church and be prophetic about it. This could be especially true when practicing in areas less affluent than the United States of America under the auspices of an American denomination. For example, Frisch (1991) has suggested specific areas of intervention with individuals, groups, and families in a Guatemalan Indian village. One is left with the impression that an American denomination sponsoring Frisch's ministry could be challenged to advocate for changes in U.S. international policies affecting the Guatemalan people.

One of the major obstacles could be the insistence of the church on a monolithic organizational arrangement which precludes the desirable exchange of energy with its immediate cultural environment. In this regard, it can be argued that Jesus' intention was for his church to remain as a social movement, a continued spiritual awakening and social renovation for the human race, a promoter of a new social order. Should the church have remained as a social movement instead of a formal organization, the church would have been free to maintain its prophetic voice against oppressive dominant groups and its capacity for self-renewal without alienating itself from the world. Church social work, applied theology, could be the means to recapture that original element of social radicalism. The church hesitates, at times, to fulfill its social agenda in its unwillingness to challenge the established order. When the church has been able to question the official definition of justice, the church has sided with the oppressed. Let us consider two contemporary examples.

The African-American church has been a determinant factor in the civil rights movement of the United States of America. Aldon Morris (1984) has documented that the infrastructure of the movement was a church-related organization under the auspices of the African-American church.

The second example: Southside Presbyterian church in Tucson, Arizona, and five California churches gave birth to the sanctuary movement in 1982 (Golden and McConnell, 1986). Originally, the movement challenged the position of the U.S. Department of Justice in regard to refugees from El Salvador. By January 1985 a federal grand jury in Phoenix had indicted 16 persons, among them five ministers of religion.

Social relevance compels the church into a constant self-denying attitude in behalf of those members of the human race who have been stripped of their self confidence and human dignity (Chikane, 1990). In this sense, church instrumentality not only implies the expression of God's purpose; it also confronts humanity with God's purpose. It insists on a human response to God's agony materialized in the plight of that sector of God's creation that has been labeled the oppressed.

Conclusion

Social work practice in an international setting offers a unique opportunity to engage the church in a self-evaluative journey. Before this can be accomplished, the worker will need to be familiar with the biblical basis upon which the task of the church rests and to have a working knowledge of Third World theologians (see recommended sources).

The original intentions of Jesus for the church were to continue his efforts toward a new social order where justice would prevail. This social order would most likely be constantly in collision with the established order. Therefore, the church needs to be structurally flexible and philosophically uncompromising, so that it is able: (1) to be sensitive to its time and space; (2) to keep a sense of instrumentality, seeking the improvement of the quality of life not only of its membership, but those outside; and (3) to become the promoter and preserver of the unity of the human race with itself and its Creator.

By utilizing this tridemensional model for practice, social workers engaged in church-related organizations overseas may contribute to the church's own spiritual journey, a journey committed to the oppressed of the land.

NOTES

[1] For the use of general systems theory in the social sciences, see Ludwing von Bertalanffy (1968) *General system theory foundations, development, applications.* Revised Edition. New York: George Braziller.

[2] The emphasis of John 17:18 and 20:21 is to Jesus' desire for his church to provide continuity to the Father's purpose which he, Jesus, had initiated.

[3] For a provocative reflection on the here-and-nowness of the church, see Bishop Pedro Casaldaliga (1988), *In pursuit of the kingdom*, chapter V. Maryknoll: Orbis.

[4] Praxis may be defined as the tangible expression of faith.

[5] See the National Association of Social Workers (NASW) *Code of Ethics,* IV, 3 and VI 1-3.

[6] Ample illustrations may be found in a very revealing series of ancient documents on the Christianization process of Latin America. These documents have been edited by H. M. Godpasture (1989). *Cross and swords: An eyewitness history of christianity in Latin America.*

[7] This is especially true when the denominational tendency is to dichotomize the task of the church: evangelism and social work, or material needs and spiritual needs. For example, see Delos Miles (1988), Church social work and evangelism: Partners in ministry. *Review and Expositor.* 85, 2, 273-283.

[8] The term means *Mother and Teacher.* It is also the name of a Papal encyclic promulgated by John XXIII in 1961.

[9] Vertical integration is the ability of an industrial complex to own the different stages undergone by a finished product. For example, a corporate farm may own the land, the cattle, the feed producing laboratory, heavy transportation equipment to transport the animals, the slaughtering facility, and the meat processing facilities.

[10] For an enlightening discussion on social work technology transfer, see P. Chatterjee and H. Ireyes (1981). Technology transfer. *International Social Work,* 24, 1, 14-22.

For a discussion on comparative ideas on social welfare, see N.W.S Chow (1987). Western and Chinese ideas of social welfare. *International Social Work,* 30, 1, 31-42.

For an educational agenda on cross-cultural social work practice, see Garland and Escobar (1988). Education for cross-cultural social work practice. *Journal of Social Work Education,* 24, 3, 229-241.

[11] According to Makhanya (1990), original Christian missions and colonizing efforts were partners in the promotion of racial segregation in South Africa. See G. Makhanya (1990). History of the Baptists convention of Southern Africa. In Hoffmeister and Gurney (1990) (Eds.) *The Barkly West national awareness workshop,* pp. 33-41. Johannesburg: Awareness Campaign Committee of the Baptist Convention of South Africa.

[12] Recently, CSWE executive director, D. Beless, challenged social work educators "to lead the profession back into the mainstream of public sector services." See *Social Work Education Reporter* (May 1991), 39.

[13] For example, *Spirituality and Social Work Communicator* (SSWC) is the newsletter published by a network of social work scholars. The network has the ambitious plan "to stimulate the social work profession to play an important and creative part in the spiritual development of local, national, and global levels of the human community." *SSWC,* 1 (2) Summer 1990.

REFERENCES

Alves, R. (1984). *What is religion?* Maryknoll: Orbis.

Boff L. (1989). *Faith on the edge.* San Francisco: Harper & Row.

Boesak, A. (1977). *Farewell to innocence: A socio-ethical study on black theology and power.* Maryknoll: Orbis.

Casaldiga, B.P. (1990). *In pursuit of the kingdom.* Maryknoll: Orbis.

Chatterjee, P. and Ireyes, H. (1981). Technology transfer implications for social work practice and social work education. *International Social Work*, 24, 1, 14-22.

Chikane, F. (1990). Knowing the truth in an oppressive system. In Hoffmeister, D. and Gurney, B.J. (1990) (Eds.), *The Barkly West national awareness workshop.* Johannesburg: Awareness Campaign Committee of the Baptist Convention of S.A.

Comblin, J. (1979), *The church and national security state.* Maryknoll: Orbis.

Cnaan, R. A. (1988). Social services for the enemy? Education for social work and the Arab sector in Israel. *International Social Work*, 31, 6, 33-44.

Culto Cristiano. New York: El Escudo. 1964.

Dussel, E. (1978). *Ethics and the theology of liberation.* Maryknoll: Orbis.

Escobar, D. (1988). International church social work: A functional component in foreign missions. *Review and Expositor*, 85, 2, 291-296.

Frisch, D. (1991). *Church social work in the third world: A model for practice within an aldea in a Guatemalan Indian community.* Unpublished MSW project, The Southern Baptist Theological Seminary, Carver School of Social Work, Louisville, KY.

Garland, D.S.R. (1988). The church as a context for social work practice. *Review and Expositor*, 85, 2, 255-265.

Garland, D.R. and Escobar, D. (1988). Education for cross-cultural social work practice. *Journal of Social Work Education*, 24, 3, 229-241.

Golden, R. and McConnell, M. (1986). *Sanctuary: The new underground railroad.* Maryknoll: Orbis.

Goodpasture, H.M. (1989). *Cross and sword.* Maryknoll: Orbis.

Gutierrez, G. (1985). *We drink from our own wells: The spiritual journey of a people.* Maryknoll, Orbis.

Gutierrez, G. (1988). *A theology of liberation history, politics, and salvation.* Revised Edition. Maryknoll: Orbis.

100

Himnario Bautista, Segunda Edicion. (1978) El Paso: Casa Bautista de Publicaciones.

Hoffmeister, D. and Gurney, B.J. (1990). *The Barkly West national awareness workshop.* Johannesburg: The Awareness Campaign Committee of the Baptist Convention of Southern Africa.

Miles, D. (1988). Church social work and evangelism: Partners in ministry. *Review and Expositor.* 85, 2, 273-283.

Morris, A. (1984). The origins of the civil rights movement. New York: Free Press.

Neuhous, R. I. (1977). Christian faith and public policy. Minneapolis: Augsburg.

Patel, L. (1987). Towards a critical theory and practice in social work with special reference to South Africa. *International Social Work*, 29, 3, 21-236.

Quiroz-Martin, T. (1986). Latin American reality and social work. *International Social Work*, 29, 2, 111-122.

Roan, S.S. (1980). Utilizing traditional elements in the society in casework practice. *International Social Work*, 23, 4, 26-35.

Romo, O. (1982). Language Mission Annual Conference of National Consultants. Unpublished material.

Shorter, A. (1977). *African Christian theology: Adaptation or incarnation.* Maryknoll: Orbis.

Tamaez, E. (1982). *Bible of the oppressed.* Maryknoll: Orbis.

Tutu, D. (1984). *Hope and suffering: Sermons and speeches.* Grand Rapids, Eerdmans.

Webster J. (1982). *Crying in the wilderness.* Grand Rapids: Eerdmans.

Yoder, J.H. (1972). *The politics of Jesus.* Grand Rapids: William B. Eerdmans.

OTHER RECOMMENDED SOURCES

Boff, L. (1978). *Ecclesiogenesis: The base communities reinvent the church.* Maryknoll: Orbis.

Erdozain, P. (1980). *Archbishop Romero: Martyr of Salvador.* Maryknoll: Orbis.

Boesak, A. (1982). *The finger of god: Sermons on faith and socio-political responsibility.* Maryknoll: Orbis.

Koyama, K. (1974). *Waterbuffalo theology.* Maryknoll: Orbis.

Ellis, M. H. and Maduro, O. (1990). *Expanding the view: Gustavo Gutierrez and the future of liberation theology.* Maryknoll: Orbis.

CHAPTER 7

Social Action and the Church

by Janet F. Spressart*

Social Action and Its Definition

As she closed her stirring address to the 1988 convention of the North American Association of Christians in Social Work, advocate Nancy Amidei told of going one day to visit an Episcopal priest whom she admires enormously for all the things he has done for poor people. As she made her way to his office, she passed a mountain of donated clothes, stacks of donated food and a bulletin board with sign-up sheets for a variety of emergency services, including such things as housing, transportation, and child care. Walking into the priest's office, she suggested that he rename the church the Emergency Episcopal Church. It was truly an amazing place!

He responded, "Don't you be fooled. If I wanted to be sure that the good people of this country did nothing about social justice, I'd put a thousand hungry people on their doorstep, and you know what those good Christian people would do? Why, they'd organize a food drive, they'd organize people to donate food, they'd organize people to pick up the food, they'd organize the people to store the food, to stack it and take it down, open it up, cook it and serve it. They'd even organize the people to clean up after the food had been eaten. They'd be so busy moving those cans from one end of town to the other they wouldn't have any time left to do anything about why those people were hungry in the first place."

The priest knew that the micro focus displayed by his parishioners resulted in short-term change for those who benefited from the most sincere of efforts. He longed for his community to evidence a response to the broader issues with the same fervor and ardent activity. Perhaps he shared with Pericles, famous philosopher of 430 B.C., the concern that the macro focus not be abandoned. It was Pericles' belief that "the real disgrace of poverty (is) not in owning to the fact but in declining the struggle against it" (Furness, 1972, p. 63).

*Janet F. Spressart, ACSW, is Statewide Director of Programs and Children's Mental Health Advocate, Mental Health Association, New Jersey.

Whether the issue at hand is one of poverty, racism, abortion, housing, equality of education, ageism, stigma against mental illness, or one of the countless others which vie for the public's attention, the existence of this healthy tension argues that choices must be made concerning the forum for that struggle. The micro focus maintains a level of social interaction where the helper enables the individuals or the group to affect the change on a personal basis. The macro focus, know as social action, influences change in social policy where systems are ultimately driven by the values and norms of society at large. The personal impact of such change is not likely to be felt as quickly by the disenfranchised or oppressed groups who may ultimately receive its benefits.

Social action is the term applied to the strategies directed toward social change. It is an inseparable element in social work, although not unique to the profession. Social action efforts are undertaken by representatives of many disciplines and communities in order to meet human needs and improve social functioning (Thursz, 1977, p. 1276). Increasingly evident in the movements which bring about change has been the participation of the consumers or beneficiaries of the espoused change. Understanding social action as a viable component within the framework of Christianity and the context of church social work provides the impetus for this final chapter.

Biblical Historical Perspective

Christians in social work recognize God's action in lives where, by the Spirit, change takes place in the ways people interact with God, with each other, and with society. God has been socially active historically, a reality which gives confidence to God's people today as they seek God's mind and direction concerning carrying out God's agenda. Not only is there Biblical evidence of God's relationships with individuals, but the Scriptures document God's intervention on behalf of nations where God's leaders, strategically placed, played key roles in producing change in social conditions.

For example, a conceited teenaged boy named Joseph, sold into slavery by his jealous brothers, later served directly under Pharoah to administer famine relief during one of the earliest recorded food distribution programs (Genesis 37-47). Another record reflects the courage of beautiful Queen Esther, whose willingness to put her life on the line for her nation was honored by her king and by the salvation of her nation from the bigotry of the unscrupulous Hamaan (Esther 3-7).

Other Old Testament sources remind us that revival always sets the stage for social action, as under Asa who brought about religious reforms at a time when the young Kingdom of Judah needed to be directed to seek the Lord (2 Chronicles 15:2-15). Under Jehoshaphat, a notable result was the education of the people in the godly life (2 Chronicles 17:1-10). The Jehoiada-Joash renewal emphasized God's primacy in the political life (2 Chron. 23:16-21; 24:1). Wide-sweeping changes under Hezekiah resulted in focus on personal sanctification with restoration of national spiritual objectives (2 Chron. 29:3-36; 30:1-26). Under Josiah, national obedience to God was highlighted with results in many areas of social relationships (2 Chron. 34:3-33; 35:1-19). Revival under Nehemiah produced political, religious and social improvements (Nehemiah, chapters 8, 9, 10). Isaiah and Amos, among other prophets, record the Lord's words requiring that Israel "learn to do right! Seek justice, encourage the oppressed. Defend the cause of the fatherless; plead the case of the widow" (Isaiah 1:17).

Our Lord enunciated a philosophy in direct opposition to the social system which existed when He was on earth. From the human perspective, He paid the highest price in order to effect change. His victory over death gives hope to all who follow that the future will see the establishment of the social system reflective of His divine nature characterized by peace, love, unity, equality, and justice. In the meantime, He sent His Spirit to empower His people to continue the work of making all men and women disciples.

Church History Perspective

Both Solomon and James wrote of God's admonitions to the Israelites that they care for their own people, including strangers and aliens. Proverbs 3:27-28 declares, "Do not withhold good from whose who deserve it, when it is in your power to act. Do not say to your neighbor, 'Come back later. I'll give it tomorrow' when you now have it with you." James' epistle reads, "Suppose a brother or sister is without clothes and daily food. If one of you says to him, 'Go, I wish you will, keep warm and well fed,' but does nothing about his physical needs, what good is it? In the same way, faith by itself, if it is not accompanied by action, is dead." (James 2:16-17, *NIV*).

If under the law it was the expected thing to help all comers in need when possible to do so, certainly under grace the Christian obligation is to do at least that much. The Apostle Paul wrote with similar intent to the Galatians. "As we have opportunity, let us do good to all people, especially to those who belong to the family of believers" (Gal. 6:10, *NIV*). The family of believers may be those attending one's local church or may be believers in the Church Universal who, as members of God's family by faith in Jesus, suffer as a result of sin's destruction in this world. God's people spurred on to social action never realize the full impact their endeavors may have on members of the family of believers, nor, for that matter, on the human family in general.

Bruce Larson writes in his study of the acts of the apostles, *Wind and Fire* (1984), that in order to be authentic apostolic people, we must carry out a fourfold commission:

> First of all, we are evangelists. We are called to tell the Good News wherever we go . . . . Second, apostolic people are involved in ministry. We're called to be those who love, affirm, heal, bless, and encourage one another in Jesus' name . . . . Third, apostolic people are on mission. We bring the good news from Jerusalem to Rome and we bring it to those at home as well. . . . Finally, apostolic people are involved in prophecy. Prophecy takes place when the people of God speak out about the evil and injustices and inadequacies of the structures and institutions of society. Prophecy means calling for new approaches to law or to health care or to government or penology or education (1984, pp. 19-20).

Against such a backdrop, powerful revival movements throughout history have been characterized both by spiritual awakening and effective social action. Evidence abounds that they have been consistently closely aligned, perhaps to the point where one would have been ineffectual without the other. According to sociologist David Moberg: Evangelical Christianity was a major influence in many social reforms in industrial societies during the eighteenth and nineteenth centuries. It had a profound impact on the abolition movement, prison reform, the treatment of the mentally ill, and working conditions of industrial laborers in England. The concern of evangelicals for human needs led to the establishment of many welfare societies which helped to alleviate the effects of social ills. Much zealous concern for social welfare can be traced to the compassion originally awakened by revivalists for sinning and suffering men (1965, p. 17).

Examples of persons whose powerful influence changed history endure. John Wesley fought the slave trade, beverage alcohol, and abuse of the poor. William Wilberforce, as a member of Parliament, crusaded for twenty years against slavery in the United Kingdom, a crusade fueled by the preaching of Charles Finney, the famous nineteenth-century evangelist who aided the underground railroad. Timothy Dwight, while president of Yale, worked for women's rights and struggled against racial discrimination (Pinson, 1975, p. 35). Evangelists themselves, such as Dwight L. Moody, preached against conditions which left the poor to suffer and which discriminated against the disadvantaged. Billy Sunday opposed alcohol and oppression of the poor by the rich. Charles Spurgeon courageously tackled such issues as slavery, war, unjust labor conditions, and poverty. Dorothea Dix championed the care of the mentally ill in prison, endeavoring to treat them differently than the convicts, but losing no opportunity to strive for prison reform in order to more humanely care for the prisoners.

Social change in America has been spurred on by organized religion. Revolution's success turned ministers and laymen to issues of guarantees for religious liberty and separation of church and state. Times of war were often viewed as holy crusades. Churches have led the struggles for economic justice, labor reform, prohibition, civil rights and against gambling, pornography, pollution and war. And the church gained its great strength for these battles on its knees, fueling action with prayer.

When commitment to social change required more than the local church resources would allow, organizations began to develop to serve in association with the local church. More than a century ago, rescue missions began to provide housing and food for transient men whose lives were profoundly disrupted by the economic upheavals of the day. These para-church organizations served on behalf of the local church bodies who were unable to be present in the most difficult sections of cities or to serve the neediest persons day after day. Today, rescue missions continue as arms of the local church, representing Christian ministry by providing innovative and timely services. The volunteer efforts of members of local churches energize these inner city mission ministries. Rescue mission staff personnel are qualified in many areas to provide valuable one-on-one services to men, women and children confronting crises of health, housing and relationships. At the same time, mission leaders supply the backbone of many social action efforts within American's cities, including improvement of conditions for the homeless, provision of medical care for the indigent, and reform of prison and welfare systems.

Social Work's Social Action Focus

During the same era when rescue missions developed, social work was becoming an established and identifiable vocation. This was due largely to the fertile environment for social reform which existed at the turn of the century. Social work's primary strategy had been individual case advocacy rather than class advocacy, but the growth of the Charity Organization Society in Boston and Jane Addam's Settlement Movement in Chicago moved individual needs into the context of communities, converting them from private troubles to public issues (Haynes & Mickelson, 1991).

Social work's attention to social action fluctuated, dependent upon the current winds of world conflict or developments within the profession. During periods of war, the profession appeared to focus inwardly, developing its clinical identity during World War I, its professionalism during World War II and the Korean conflict, and its efficiency and accountability during the Viet Nam years. Whenever domestic crises mounted, however, social work seemed to soar to advanced level of involvement. The New Deal's response to the Great Depression engaged the young profession in early coalition experiences born out of widespread recognition of social problems and simultaneous identification of the public's responsibility.

Late in the 1950s, social work's energy turned to civil rights injustices and opposition to the Cold War's arms race. The early and dramatic days of America's new Frontier and War on Poverty confronted social work with the opportunity to develop objective and rational beliefs which propelled the profession into the essential and unquestionable social action arena. The endurance gained during the arduous '60s served as the profession's boot camp for the crushing frustrations of the next two decades. The policies of New Federalism reduced, as if by major surgery, the resources government had committed to numerous services and programs for the disadvantaged. Social workers, many of whom recognized for the first time the essential nature of social action as it related to empowering the disenfranchised, also discovered that many of their fellow professionals were not even registered voters and were thus unable to participate in changing the system at the most elementary level (Haynes & Mickelson, 1991).

As part of its professional mission, the National Association of Social Workers developed a lobbying branch called ELAN (Education Legislation Action Network) and a branch working for the election of pro-human services candidates known as PACE (Political Action for Candidate Endorsement). Any political activity remains a matter of individual preference and is even subject to "opposition from peers who view social action as a degrading deprofessionalization of social work" (Haynes & Mickelson, 1991, p. 11). This ambivalence has raised strong discussions relative to what might be the best manner to train social workers regarding social action.

The Context for Today's Social Action

The development of social work as a ministry component within the church has not been free from similar debate as it relates to the appropriate nature of social action in this context. In his book *Applying the Gospel*, William Pinson, Jr. cites several objections which have prevailed against social action efforts by church groups. Fear of change, of causing controversy and conflict, of having to face individual vested interests and prejudices compounded with lack of understanding of human need and suffering pose formidable barriers (Pinson, 1975). Then there were those who became concerned that attention to social ills would detract from the more essential preaching of the gospel and from maintaining the supremacy of the authoritative scriptures in an age when the integrity of the Bible was being threatened on every hand. Sherwood Wirt reflected that "the weakness of the Bible defender of the recent past was not so much his premises or his logic as his failure to look out for the needs of his neighbor. He was too often blinded by all the smoke from the theological brush fires and unable to see what was happening to his world. The social conscience of the evangelical went into rigor mortis" (Wirt, 1968, p. 46). The unfortunate result of this state was the lack of contact Bible reading followers of Jesus actually maintained with the people Jesus had called them to serve.

Overwhelming social upheaval in the second half of the twentieth century has created an environment so intense that followers of Jesus cannot deny the opportunities which require social action responses. No longer has there been energy for arguments which divide the spiritual need from the social reality. Instead, a renewed awareness now underlies the restoration of Christian social action. This awareness addresses concern for the whole of a human being, very much in the context of holistic practice. In understanding individuals' potential for completeness in our Lord Jesus Christ, social action embodies a commitment to compassion and servanthood which demands ministry of the whole gospel, a prophetic vision which transforms society, changes the landscape, brings down kings and rebuilds highways (Ward, 1983).

Such commitment does not move at whim but as the result of planned change. Unlike social reform or social revolution which occur by sheer force of events without deliberate human planning, social action is best understood when each social act comprising it is analyzed, each cause of each act understood, and responsibility for each act determined. Using this procedure in planning any social action before it is carried out might well prevent ill-advised and unjustified action (Furness, 1972, p. 28).

Without purposeful planning, the action is likely not to make a difference. The very presence of Jesus on earth was part of a purposeful sovereign plan with the view toward making a difference. Any church which launches a social action effort will maintain this view and monitor its steps accordingly.

Three models may be applied to social workers who initiate social action efforts toward the achievement of social change. Potential for the application of any of these models exists in the context of the local church.

The first model is of *the citizen social worker*, one who confronts social issues as a citizen, not within the context of professional obligation but as a representative who brings information gained from working with individuals and groups.

The social change agent represents the second model by purposefully directing social action toward change. A number of well developed theoretical systems may be used to achieve desired results. These might include active participation in the political processes of an organization or system, entrance into the political arena to deal more effectively with the community's structure, or response to the status quo by mobilizing in what might be perceived to be a negative fashion through the use of protests or strikes. Such methods may disrupt routine functions of the community or organization in order to call public attention to a cause, but would not be organized to include violence for the accomplishment of the same purpose.

On the other hand, there are occasions when civil disobedience may be employed "as a means to register public defiance of a law or policy which is enforced by established governmental authorities, insofar as the action is premeditated, understood to be illegal or of contested legality and carried out for limited public ends through carefully chosen and limited means" (Haynes & Mickelson, p. 11). Of civil disobedience, Pinson writes:

> Faced with an immoral law, a Christian citizen has a responsibility to refuse to obey that law while recognizing the right of government to punish such disobedience. In an act of civil disobedience a person publicly breaks a law in order to arrested so that the law can be tested in the courts or public opinion aroused against it. The goal is to get a particular law changed or social practice altered; in this sense, civil disobedience differs from a crime in which a person secretly breaks the law for

personal, selfish advantage. Most Christians believe civil disobedience should be non-violent (1975, pp. 81 & 82).

The third model is embodied in *the actionist* who believes that social change for the disenfranchised can only be achieved by developing and using political, economic or social pressure. Here, confrontation and bargaining are viewed as the best methods for bringing about social change. The needs of the group on whose behalf the actionist is engaged win priority in all negotiations. The sanction of the group with which the actionist is identified matters more than the sanction of the profession or the community at large from which the actionist originates (Haynes & Mickelson, pp. 9 & 10). This model produces empowered consumers of human services.

Advocacy has emerged as an essential element of social action and can be applied to any of the three models mentioned previously. From the Latin *ad vocare*, the word means to speak for or plead the cause of another, with roots deeply entrenched in biblical history and prophecy, this concept of striving to make others care on behalf of those who are unheard or unseen is a valued component of responsible social action endeavors. Advocacy requires being informed, articulating testimony in public and political arenas, understanding who is responsible for affecting change in relationship to an issue, writing letters and communicating with policy makers and their staff, and persistently working toward goals. Advocates attack problems, not people, and a clear understanding of legitimate rights pervades all of the advocate's functions. In the end, the advocate's work is to accomplish what the client wants in a manner which will empower the client and which will not be energized by what the advocate wants to do for the client, regardless of how noble.

The Contemporary Church Chooses Social Action

The urban crises of the sixties revealed the absence of interventions, Christian or otherwise. Since then, American's cities have been a focal point of revived social action efforts. At that time, many churches had left the crumbling cities rather than redesign their identity of ministry to reflect changing contexts. Churches which remained were often confronted by their own entrenched attitudes concerning the people and the problems in the cities. Cold, stone edifices became monuments to religious influences of the past while storefront churches embodied the dynamic of the city at worship.

Much of the renewed interest in urban social action was driven by efforts of groups which functioned alongside the church or with a view toward specialized ministry. Parachurch organizations have long existed to carry on specialized ministries to some particular segment of the city. Charles Colson reminds us that "feeding the hungry did not originate with Live-Aid. Christians have been doing it since the church began . . . . Organizations such as World Vision, Catholic Relief Services and the Salvation Army have for generations been feeding the hungry, housing the homeless and clothing the needy without the glamorous carrot-and-stick razzle-dazzle so recently discovered by the rich and famous" (1987, p. 254).

Frank R. Tillapaugh writes in *Unleashing the Church*,

The local church has a lot to learn from parachurch groups. Back in the early forties, God gave Dawson Trotman a burning desire to reach sailors for Christ. Out of his ministry came the present-day worldwide ministry of the Navigators. It's not shameful that Trotman founded the Navigators. In fact, the entire evangelical community can rejoice that this superb ministry came into being. It is regrettable, however, that Trotman *had* to bypass the church to have an effective ministry with sailors. It wasn't possible to minister to sailors in the majority of local churches in the 1940s nor is it possible today. This raises a serious question: Why must people bypass the church to minister to many of the groups in our culture? (1982, p. 15).

In recent years, parachurch organizations have responded to that question by linking their unique opportunities for social action with the mission of local church outreach. This design flourished under ministries of such organizations as Prison Fellowship and Habitat for Humanity. These groups and others provided for society's inspection and participation creative means to alter conditions for the suffering.

Prison Fellowship is the first full-scale assault by the Christian church on America's prisons in this century. Born out of Chuck Colson's promise to fellow inmates not to forget them when he was released in 1979, its ministry now harnessess the efforts of thousands of volunteers in communities around the world and from churches of all denominations. Individual counseling, Bible study fellowship groups, linkages with family on the outside, and advocacy for change within prisons and the systems of which they are a part all transpire with resounding impact on behalf of prisoners on every continent today.

Habitat for Humanity is a non-profit ecumenical Christian organization, based in Americus, Georgia, with more than 500 affiliates in North America which have been involved in building projects in 31 nations. Volunteers work side by side with needy people in constructing or renovating dwellings that they will ultimately own and occupy. Prospective homeowners contribute hundreds of hours of "sweat equity in their new homes, which are purchased for the cost of construction with interest-free mortgages provided by Habitat. Using the philosophy that "a hand up is not a handout," Habitat for Humanity accomplishes its task among the underprivileged by enlisting volunteers from local churches.

Such para-church examples highlight the impact of single-focus ministries which address specific social issues. However, the impact of a local church which actively responds to the pain of its own people, the suffering of its own community, and the needs of its own neighborhood is unquestionable. This response need not neglect the spiritual ministries of the church but is essentially linked with the ministries of evangelism and Christian nurturing.

Social action as an organizational function of the church or denomination often finds substance in statements of social issues. To develop statements or positions which become public requires that local churches be knowledgeable about those social issues.

> Public responsibility includes . . . the question of the responsibility of the church as an influence on the moral and social influences confronting society. The church should clearly delineate its stand on . . . public issues . . . . It may choose to take no stand at all, but it should do so as a matter of decision and not as a result of apathy (Kilinski and Wofford, 1973, pp. 139-140).

In order for today's church to maintain a practicable social action ministry, priorities are necessary. No church can possibly meet all the needs which may be present in its community. Pinson suggests a few test questions by which a church might determine its priorities for action:

1. Which social problems affect the most people in our community?
2. Which problems are the most seriously damaging to human life?
3. Which needs are being dealt with in the least adequate way by other groups?
4. Which problems are we best equipped to handle in light of our resources?
5. Which needs do we feel God is leading us to deal with? (1975, p. 82)

In *The Christian and Social Action,* Charles Furness delineated three useful guidelines for assessing the projects and evaluating the energy which might be required to carry out action efforts.

1. The Christian should [be involved] in real and urgent situations which it is clearly the business of the church and its members to

do something about, providing they have the ability and personnel to do the work.

2. The Christian should not succumb to the temptation to dabble in other issues which would not be of the nature of clear need and calling for immediate action. Also, he should not manufacture or force crises simply to keep stirred up by a feeling that he must always be engaged in social action or be disobedient if he is not.

3. There are enough chronic social ills present and continuing, like poverty and the harm it does to the many poor, to give reason for ongoing action ministries between emergencies (1972, p. 241-242).

Models of Action

The church in the twentieth century has responded to a multitude of opportunities for social action. Denominations have launched effective ministries which have become models world wide. At the same time, local churches have seized moments of opportunity to act on behalf of the social needs in their communities with no less profound success. Consider the following examples.

SHARE began as a local ministry of the Order of St. Vincent de Paul in a parish located on the west coast of the United States. Today it has grown to international proportions, a non-profit organization of the Catholic Church which maintains dignity for the hungry while endeavoring to feed them. SHARE provides thirty to thirty-five pounds of groceries per month to underprivileged persons who pay $13, with the remaining spent for administrative costs. Large contributions of food are made by corporations and suppliers. The presence of SHARE in neighborhoods across America and increasingly in location in Europe and South America gives families who would face the distress of hunger the ability to participate in helping themselves and their communities.

Three Grace Brethren churches in Philadelphia, Pennsylvania represent a small but increasingly urban-sensitive fellowship of churches. Three visionary pastors live in different neighborhoods of the city amid gangs, drugs, murders, robberies, poverty, cockroaches and homeless youth. One church purchased an old legion post building nearby, refurbishing it into a community center. Its main function is to provide a place where kids can go to get off the street. Another church envisions the creation of a full-service community center offering counseling, drug and alcohol rehabilitation and vocational training. All three churches find the greatest social action effort comes from simply engaging their people in learning the skills of talking with people who might otherwise feel that the church has no interest in their practical needs (Inner City Ministries, 1991).

For Budd Lake Community Chapel, a non-denominational church in rural northern New Jersey, social action came in the form of radical hospitality when the pastor and his wife turned their home into Barachah Barn. David and Ruth Rupprecht, along with four other families, launched a ministry to rebellious teens, battered women, abandoned children, and others in need of temporary shelter by responding to Jesus' words to His host:

> Then Jesus said to his host, 'When you give a luncheon or din-
> ner, do not invite your friends, your brothers or relatives, or your
> rich neighbors; if you do, they may invite you back and so you
> will be repaid. But when you give a banquet, invite the poor, the
> crippled, the lame, the blind, and you will be blessed. Although
> they cannot repay you, you will be repaid at the resurrection of
> the righteous.' (Luke 14:12-14).

In order to bring to fruition God's plan to "set the lonely in families" (Ps 68:6), radical hospitality required that open Christian homes "where family members are consciously working at their relationships to the Lord God and to each other" be available "to someone who has been torn emotionally or relationally by sin or others, so that he or she can see first hand the power of God to redeem, change and heal" (Rupprecht, 1983, p. 14).

Radical hospitality is not, as its name might more commonly imply, an extreme form of social action. Rather, in keeping with an accurate defini- tion of terms, "radical" means going to the center, the foundation or source in this case, of meeting human need by providing what is basic. To be successful, radical hospitality involves three components. First, mature, stable families are led by the Holy Spirit's power. Second, the local church provides support to the families and to those whom they serve through prayer and material assistance. Third, the bruised in- dividual benefits from time in a place of refuge while they work toward the goal of reunification with family or develop the means to find new independence. "Scripture has given a basis for the ministry of radical hospitality; society has accentuated the need; the Christian church is now called to action so that bruised reeds may grow tall and dim wicks may burn bright once more" (Rupprecht, 1983, p. 29).

Helping the disadvantaged discover the benefits of permanent hous- ing, St. Joseph's Parish in East Camden, New Jersey is committed to providing home ownership opportunities to people who otherwise could not afford them. In the past five years, financial and technical assistance offered by parish volunteers and staff, in partnership with the New Jersey Department of Community Affairs, has enabled 30 families in one of the state's most depressed areas to move toward the enjoyment of affordable home ownership.

A most dynamic example of Christian social action began in the grass roots ministry which became known as Voice of Calvary under the leadership of John Perkins in Jackson and Mendenhall, Mississippi. This multifaceted, racially integrated ministry includes basic health care, essentials of early education, and the development of a cooperative store, all of which direct social action to health care, education and economic crises the poor face in those communities. John Perkins had formulated a practical basis for change which he now calls the three Rs of community development: *relocation*–actually being located as a helper where the need exists, *reconciliation*–changing long standing hostilities and broken relationships through healing and forgiveness, and *redistribution* –serving people with the shared resources of technology, education and skills. Organized tutoring, adult education, leadership training and health services characterize this thriving ministry which has had impact, not only on the local community, but on communities throughout the nation where the model has been employed.

Other models abound: A church in Flemington, New Jersey mobilized the community against the presence of an adult pornography store and won a court injunction to keep it closed. St. Francis Table is a non-profit diner in Toronto where the needy may eat for one dollar; they are served by parish volunteers who include senior citizens, the working poor, single parents and persons appointed to accomplish acts of community service by the justice system. Churches in the New York Metropolitan area collaborated to organize a clothing drive for families of a city community which was destroyed by fire during winter holidays. It becomes difficult to distinguish between simple acts of service and those which strategically address planned social change. The very act of service can be part of such a strategy and certainly provides credibility for continuing action efforts.

Social action for church communities often finds expression in united efforts among groups who share a common passion in some area of social need. Frequently church groups struggle with the question of how closely identified their social action can and should be with denominations of diverse theological identity. This remains a matter which fellowships of churches and denominational entities determine as opportunities arise. In order to provide a broad and unified voice with significant visibility based on common doctrinal distinctives, organizations such as the *National Association of Evangelicals* and *Evangelicals for Social Action* represent the social concerns of affiliates at the federal level.

Similar power may be created through local coalition efforts. For instance, the Newark-North Jersey Committee of Black Churchmen represents 250 churches in coalition with other advocacy organizations in New Jersey to increase the state's standard of need for families at the poverty level. Their pressure on the system led to the achievement of a process which had not been addressed for at least ten years. Now the Committee leads its crusade to increase the monthly grant by at least $300 each month in order for families to sustain an adequate life. Their strategy calls for the government to stop subsidizing 80-dollar-a-night rodent and drug infested motel rooms for homeless families. They believe those dollars can be spent on decent apartments with money remaining to raise welfare grants. Their call to utilize resources already in the system conforms to the present fiscal environment and in coalition with Legal Services, the Public Advocate and private advocacy organizations, it represents a unique social action force from the church community.

The Congregational Support Project (CSP) developed out of a concern for the mentally ill by a group which included Lutheran, United Methodist and Presbyterian clergy and lay leaders who worked with community mental health providers and state level policy makers. As mental health systems released more individuals into the ranks of the communities' displaced persons, churches needed to be prepared to respond to their needs creatively and compassionately. To that end, CSP developed a concept of church/community partnership for self-help and support. Designed to train church volunteers to facilitate opportunities for socialization and support through self-help groups and recreation, CSP efforts have resulted in the development of local caring communities which are also organized to advocate publicly for mental health appropriations and for changes in public policy. Of greater value is the empowerment of consumers of mental health services to advocate on their own behalf and to build peer support.

Perhaps no issue in this century since prohibition has sparked such heated activity as has *abortion*. Very much a moral issue as well as a social issue, strong and divergent positions have emerged among Christians. Each perspective is tied to an organization, all of which have mustered ardent action as the controversy moves toward becoming no less consuming in the next century as well. Every type of social action methodology has been called into play in defense on all sides, including

116

public testimony, demonstration, civil disobedience, letter writing, and rallies. Agreement seems unified across all perspectives, however, that the Christian community needs to maintain the right kinds of alternatives for women who are pregnant, and these must include adequate housing, health care, legal advice, job training and economic assistance.

In an effort to accomplish these goals, housing services to teen and adult women have increased, many initiated by local church efforts. The Christian Action Council's Crisis Pregnancy Center model has been reproduced hundreds of times across America. The work of CPCs proceeds primarily as a result of intensive volunteer training and is sustained by the support of area churches. The centers enlist shepherding homes to care for birth mothers and their infants after birth. In some communities, groups homes serve as maternity homes for women in waiting.

The 2 Timothy 1:7 Principle

The list of valuable social action efforts occurring in local churches today grows steadily. Confronted with the new and soon arriving twenty-first century, Christians know they have a voice and want to know how to make it heard. Most major denominations have a presence in the nation's capital to interact at the highest levels of government. Their issues include national policy regarding AIDS, health care, welfare reform, housing, child care, civil rights and education for America's children. Local community and state social action efforts are strengthened immeasureably by the maintenance of able representation at the federal front:

> The most sophisticated political activity is essential. But we must combine that political expertise with a pervasive conviction that finally the struggle belongs to God and we prevail not by might nor by power but by prayerful trust in the Sovereign of history . . . . [It] is only as the church truly models the values it proclaims that its political activity has integrity . . . . Living communities of Christians whose common life demonstrates the possibility of reconciled, just relationships between black and white, rich and poor, male and female, have a profound social impact (Sider, 1987, pp. 199-200).

Society needs Christians who move with proactive intent rather than with reactive fear. One who reacts responds only after the worst has occurred and then wonders why it happened. One who approaches life with a proactive perspective is always observing trends, relating to people,

117

never disconnected from the real world. In this way, that one becomes prepared to stand in the gap and creatively challenge the movement of history. That activity is not defensive. It is recognition of the key position Christians hold as representatives of God's action in the world. In so doing, God's people will understand existing social action issues and will determine a course of action in accordance with the Scriptures and by the leading of the Holy Spirit. They will apply knowledge of themselves, of history, of social structures, and of people and human relationships to the impelling efforts of social action.

But to what end? Charles Colson writes:

> The Kingdom of God has had . . . an astonishing effect upon the most powerful of human empires in every age. It is not a blue print for some new social order; nor does it merely set the forces of radical cultural change in motion. Rather, God's Kingdom promises radical changes in human personalities. This is the crucial point. While human politics is based on the premise that society must be changed in order to change people, in the politics of the Kingdom it is people who must be changed in order to change society.
>
> Through men and women who recognize its authority and live by its ethical standards, the Kingdom of God invades the stream of history. It breaks the vicious and otherwise irreversible cycles of violence, injustice and self-interest. In this way the Kingdom of God equips its citizens . . . to be the best citizens in the kingdoms of man (1987, p. 94).

The apostle Paul has given us a strong challenge. "For God did not give us a spirit of timidity, but a spirit of power, of love and of self-discipline" (2 Tim. 1:7, *NIV*).

References

Amidei, Nancy (September 1988). Speech delivered at Annual Convention, North American Association of Christians in Social Work, San Antonio, Texas.

Colson, Charles (1987). *Kingdoms in conflict*. New York & Grand Rapids: Morrow/Zondervan

Colson, Charles (1979). *Life sentence*. Lincoln, Virginia: Chosen Books.

Furness, Charles Y. (1972). *The Christian and social action*. Old Tappan: Revell.

Furness, Charles Y. (1978). *Helping ministries handbook: A handbook for guidance to local churches in helping ministries*. Unpublished doctoral thesis.

Haynes, Karen S. & Mickelson, James S. (1991). *Affecting change: Social workers in the political arena*. White Plains: Longman.

Holcomb, Wayne, *et al.* (1984). *Building a support system: Manual for the development of church, synagogue and mental health agency sponsored support programs for long-term recipients of mental health services*. Denville, NJ.

Inner City Ministries, Challenges of ministry and life abound for three seminary grads, (Winter, 1991). *Grace Magazine*. Winona Lake: Grace College and Theological Seminary.

Kilinski, Kenneth K., and Wofford, Jerry C. (1973). *Organization and leadership in the local church*. Grand Rapids: Zondervan.

Larson, Bruce (1984). *Wind & fire*. Waco: Word.

Moberg, David O. (1965). *Inasmuch: Christian social responsibility in the twentieth century*. Grand Rapids: Erdmanns.

New Jersey Cable Network. (March 30, 1991). Interview.

Perkins, John (1976). *A quiet revolution*. Waco: Word.

Pinson, William M., Jr. (1975). *Applying the gospel*. Nashville: Boardman.

Rupprecht, David & Ruth (1983). *Radical hospitality*. Phillipsburg: Presbyterian & Reformed Publishing.

Sider, Ron (1987). *Completely pro-life*. Downers Grove: InterVarsity.

The Star Ledger, April 28, 1991. *Teens help Habitat for Humanity build West Virginia Homes*. Newark, New Jersey.

The Star Ledger, April 22, 1991. *Advocates call welfare housing program unfair to poor and taxpayers*. Newark, NJ.

Thursz, David (1977). *Encyclopedia of social work*. Washington, DC: National Association of Social Work.

Tillapaugh, Frank R. (1982). *Unleashing the church*. Ventura: Regal.

Toronto Star, (Sept. 17, 1989). *Dollar diner serves up a new Location*. Toronto.

Ward, Dr. Ted. (1983). Seminars presented to Eastern District Conference of the International Union of Gospel Missions at America's Keswick.

Wirt, Sherwood E. (1968). *The social conscience of the evangelical*. New York: Harper and Row.

NORTH AMERICAN ASSOCIATION OF CHRISTIANS IN SOCIAL WORK

Box 7090
St. Davids, PA 19087-7090

OTHER BOOKS IN THE COLLECTION

The Poor You Have with You Always: Concepts of Aid to the Poor in the Western World, from Biblical Times to the Present (1989), 173 pages
By Alan Keith-Lucas

Encounters With Children: Stories that Help Us Understand and Help Them (1991), 35 pages
By Alan Keith-Lucas

SOCIAL WORK PRACTICE MONOGRAPH SERIES

#1: A Christian Response to Domestic Violence: A Reconciliation Model for Social Workers (1985), 44 pages
By Cathy Suttor and Howard Green

#2: So You Want to Be a Social Worker: A Primer for the Christian Student (1985; 2nd printing 1987), 35 pages
By Alan Keith-Lucas

#3: Spirit-Led Helping: A Model for Evangelical Social Work Counseling (1987), 52 pages
By William E. Consiglio